D0533452

Baby Sense

Understanding your baby's **sensory world** – the key to a contented child

Megan Faure & Ann Richardson

METZ PRESS

DEDICATION
This book is dedicated to all the 'unsettled infants' out there from
whom we've learnt so much, and who have enriched our lives
in so many ways.

Published by Metz Press
1 Cameronians Avenue, Welgemoed, 7530, South Africa

First edition 2002
   Reprinted 2003, 2004, 2005, 2006 (twice), 2007 (three times),
   2008 (twice), 2009
Second edition January 2010
   Reprinted May 2010, January 2011

Publisher & editor	Wilsia Metz
Sub-editor	Sandra Sharpe
Cover design	Liezl Marais
Design & lay-out	Lindie Metz
Illustrations	Annette van Wyk, Karmien Kruth
Index	Retha Venter
Print production	Andrew de Kock
Printing and binding	Creda Communications, Elliot Ave, Epping
ISBN	978-1-920268-64-0

Authors' acknowledgements

It has been said that it takes a village to raise a child. Well, it takes a city, then, to write a book! We want to thank all those who contributed in any way to the writing and publishing of **Baby sense.**

Writing this book began long ago with the people who impacted on the way we saw babies, their development and their difficulties. We would like to acknowledge those who taught us to look with sensory eyes: Jean Ayres, Bunty McDougall, Kerry Wallace, Kate Bailey and Georgia DeGangi.

Thank you to the many babies, children and parents in our respective practices who shared their lives and each one of whom added to the tapestry of our clinical experience.

We are indebted to many professionals for their knowledge and support without which we could not possibly have written this book. Thank you to Dr Adam Cullinan, Dr Nicole Dawson, Dr Ashley Wewege, Clare Snyman, Wynne Westaway and Lizanne Du Plessis for their professional advice; Tina Otte and Marina Petropulos for their wise words and encouragement. A special thanks must go to our esteemed colleague Dr Astrid Berg for reading our book and writing such an insightful foreword.

Thanks also to our family, friends and colleagues who endured many hours of **Baby sense** by reading and editing our early chapters more than once, who gave constructive and objective advice when asked, and who wisely kept quiet on other occasions! Elizabeth, Roeline, Jacqui, Bridget, Conny, Corinne, Michelle, Francein, Sue, Jayne, Angie and Lyn, thank you. Grateful thanks to Dave and Angie for their generous hospitality on the farm, providing the space in which to write in peace!

In the writing of this book many thanks go to Wilsia and the team at Metz Press, who believed in us, understood our passion and gave us the platform to share our ideas with the world. And to Sandra our editor who, along with Wilsia, took our 'baby', nurtured it and never let us lose sight of our vision – a book that focuses on the baby's sensory system – thank you.

And finally to our families, especially our children, James, Alexandra and Emily, Ellen and Maeve, who integrated all we ever learned about babies and development, and who have taught us the true meaning of sense-able parenting. Thank you for sharing your moms and allowing us the space to follow our dream.

And most importantly our pillars of strength: Philip and Ken. To our wonderful husbands, who brought the coffee and picked up the pieces with our children but through it all never stopped encouraging our work, our eternal gratitude and love.

Last, but by no means least, we thank our Heavenly Father for the eternal view we have of life.

Foreword

One may ask: "Do we need yet another book on baby care? Are our parents not already oversaturated with advice, with the words 'should' and 'should not'?" I am delighted to be able to say that this book is different, and that it is indeed a very necessary addition to the other books available on the subject.

Baby sense is about the baby under one year of age. That the first 12 months of life are looked at in detail is most important. All too often babies of all ages are 'lumped' together, so that no differentiation is made between the two-month-old and the 12-month-old. By staying within the first year, the time when development is at its fastest and most sensitive, the authors give this time of life the attention and priority it requires.

In our age of general over-stimulation we have come to take our infants on this fast journey too, thinking that by exposing them to all that is available we are making them brighter. Not only does much enjoyment get lost in this rush, but the over-stimulation of the immature brain can even have a damaging effect on its development. This is, to my mind, the most important message of this book: "Don't go overboard with stimulation". In a systematic and clear way the authors explain the infant's sensory experiences before birth and thereafter and then describe how this transition can be made more gently for the baby. Learning to read the baby's signals enables the parent to know when to do what in order to minimize stress.

Common problems such as colic and sleeping problems are addressed, all built on the principle that the 'sensory diet' is as fundamental to the child's development as is a nutritional diet.

The second half of the book gives details about care and development in each one of the six phases of development during the first year of life.

The balance between stimulation at the right time and calming down is emphasised throughout.

The style of writing is clear and systematic, making it also possible to use as a quick reference book. The attitude is one of flexibility and tolerance, and of accepting the individual differences that each baby and each parent bring with them. No miracle cures are given and no claims are made for perfect problem-free early months. What is offered is the possibility of looking at your baby with more sensitivity and insight, being able to understand his/her communications and basing your care-giving on the cues that are coming from your child. In the first year of life this is what is needed above all else, as the baby's signals are authentic and real.

If we as parents can truly respect our infants as individuals from the very beginning, if we can learn to observe them and understand their communications which are already quite finely developed, we will establish the foundation for good relationships for the rest of their lives.

The two authors are eminently qualified to help us with this task, as they themselves have had the best teachers: years of experience with many babies. Professionally and personally both have come to know babies of many different temperaments and have come to know the struggles of early parenthood. This enables them to look at infancy within the context of scientific knowledge and personal understanding. They thus manage to convey the 'sensible middle ground' which is so easily lost in our fast moving world.

ASTRID BERG

(Senior Child Psychiatrist, Child & Family Unit, Red Cross Children's Hospital; Senior Lecturer, Department of Psychiatry, University of Cape Town; Chairperson of the Western Cape Association of Infant Mental Health; Analyst and President of the Southern African Association of Jungian Analysts)

Contents

Three of the most common concerns of parents in their baby's first year are:
- Why is she crying?
- How can I get her to sleep well?
- How can I enhance her development?

Is it possible that the answers to all these concerns lie in one theory? We firmly believe this to be true. The key to whether your baby is happily awake, learning from her world, or falling asleep with ease and sleeping peacefully for long stretches is found in her sensory world.

The first two chapters of this book are the basis for understanding your baby's sensory world and how this affects her ability to be happily awake and fall happily asleep. **Do read them with care**.
   The rest of the book is very practical, giving guidelines and advice on using this knowledge and understanding to nurture a calm baby and at the same time enhance her development.

Our sensory world

Nothing can match that glorious moment when you hear your newborn child's first cry. Amy has just made her appearance, she draws breath for the first time and lets out a yell. Everyone present sighs with relief and joy. Through her exhaustion, Mom's tears shine on her flushed cheeks and dad experiences a rush of emotion stronger than any he had ever felt before. Amy's feelings, on the other hand, are hardly relief, joy and pride. She has just been bombarded with a barrage of sensations she didn't know existed. She sees the bright, white lights, she smells the sterile world of the labour ward and suddenly feels the light, cool touch of the air around her. Amy has made her first contact with the sensory input of the world outside the womb. The next 12 months of her life will be a gradual process of making sense of this new sensory world.

We live in a sensory-rich world. We take in information from the world through our senses and then, once the brain has integrated or processed this information, we act on it. As adults we can control to a large extent what sensory information we take in and we use that information to respond to the world or to behave in a certain way. But a baby's brain is less developed than ours. For the first few months of life your baby is unable to control what sensory information she takes in and how she responds to that information.

Understanding your young baby's immature nervous system will help you know when, why and how to nurture, stimulate or calm her. What's more, it will help you enhance her physical and mental development with controlled and appropriate stimulation, while at the same time keeping her calm and happy.

A calm and happy babyhood is not just something of convenience for parents – it is an important factor in a child's emotional development. Current thinking is that high Emotional Intelligence (EQ) is a better predictor of success and happiness in later life than a high IQ. This is discussed by Lise Eliot in her book *What's Going On In There?* (Bantam Books, 1999) – a most useful reference if you wish to delve deeper into the subject of neurological development.

SENSORY INPUT

The brain is made up of nerves. Its function is to take in information (input), decide what is important and relevant and then interpret the information so that we can perform an appropriate action in response to the input. This input is delivered to the brain by means of the senses.

Our sensory experience is not limited to input from the external world via the five senses of sight, smell, hearing, taste and touch. There are also three body senses that give information about our internal world. These are the senses of movement (vestibular sense), body position (proprioception) and information from our organs (interoception). Let's see how these senses give us a picture of the world.

- **Touch** – Our sense of touch is received from the skin and gives us information about temperature, pain, touch and pressure. When it is refined, it will tell us where we have been touched, how hard and even what we are touching. Touch gives us a sense of our bodies and tells us whether we are being threatened or comforted, so it is closely linked to our emotions.
- **Smell** – Smells are chemically perceived by receptors in the nose. Sensations from the nose are the only ones that go directly to the emotion centre in the brain, which explains why smells evoke such strong emotions and memories. We can return to childhood emotions in a flash when we encounter a smell such as the perfume our mother wore as she kissed us good night or the tempting aroma of the favourite dish our grandmother used to make.
- **Sight** – The eyes see objects, light and colour. When our sense of sight is mature we see from near to far in varying colours and we are able to perceive depth and dimension.
- **Hearing** –Sound is carried on airwaves and picked up and registered by receptors in the ear. We learn to identify where sound comes from, and then attach meaning to each sound.
- **Taste** – Taste is closely linked to smell and is chemically perceived by receptors on the tongue. Special receptors on different parts of the tongue are sensitive to salty, sour, bitter and sweet tastes respectively.
- **Movement** (vestibular sense) – Receptors in the inner ear sense changes of our position in space, more specifically, movement of our head in space. When this sense is working well, we know which direction we are moving in, how fast and whether we are speeding up or slowing down. When it functions optimally, we don't become nauseous or feel threatened by normal movement.
- **Body position** (proprioception) – Our muscles and joints give us a sense of the position of our body in space. This is important so that even without seeing our body, we know what position we're in and how our limbs are moving.
- **Interoception** – Our internal organs give us information about our comfort level and needs, such as hunger, digestion, temperature and elimination.

Receiving sensory input

Information from the senses reaches the brain via incoming sensory nerves. There are five times as many nerves in the brain devoted to receiving and organizing this sensory information than there are nerves responsible for taking action. This shows what an important role the sensory system plays.

Processing and filtering

Before we are even conscious of the sensory information received, our brain determines whether the information is important or not. If the information is not important, the brain inhibits or filters out that information by recognizing familiar input and deciding to no longer register or focus on it. This process is called

habituation. When input is habituated, it is inhibited so that it does not reach our consciousness. *For example, you are not constantly aware of the feel of your clothes on your back.* **Habituation is vital** so that we can focus on important information without becoming over-stimulated. If the process of habituation does not work properly, a great deal of unimportant information affects the system. This leads to **sensory overload or over-stimulation**.

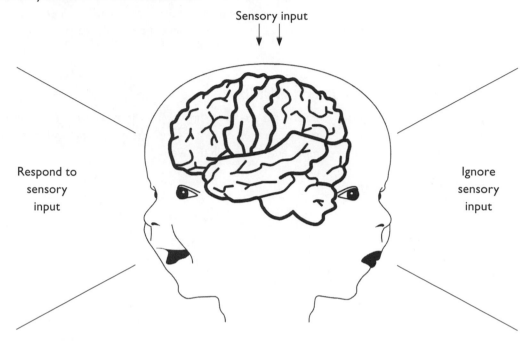

Sensory input

Respond to sensory input

Ignore sensory input

Responding

When your baby's brain perceives sensory information which is new to her or important for her to attend to, she will respond. Her response to this sensory input may be emotional, such as crying when being dressed or it may be physical, such as turning in preparation to feed when her cheek is touched by your nipple. Her responses to sensory input may be important for **learning** or **survival** or they may be **emotional**, depending on the input.

Filtering in young babies

In young babies the process of habituating or filtering sensory information is not yet mature. Your newborn will not be able to move, look away or filter strong sensory input. Even older babies and toddlers are easily over-stimulated. For this reason, in the first year of your baby's life, your nurturing role includes **filtering out excessive sensory input** to help your baby avoid sensory overload. You must regulate not only **how much** stimulation your baby receives, but also the **type** of sensory input **she is exposed to**.

You can help your baby to regulate sensory input by:
• Reading her signals indicating when she has had enough (see Chapter 4);

> A mature brain responds to important information but **habituates** irrelevant information. Your baby's brain cannot adequately habituate, so you must filter out excessive sensory input to prevent sensory overload.

- Removing her from strong sensory input when she is overloaded;
- Choosing appropriate **sensory input** which will assist her to become calm (see Chapter 2).

Each individual filters or habituates sensory information in his or her own, unique way. This explains why your baby has a different personality to another. Babies who are settled and calm are often those who filter sensory information more effectively and therefore are calmer. Other babies are very sensitive to changes in their world and these little ones are usually more alert and may be unsettled.

In time you will get to know your own little baby's temperament and how she responds to sensory information.

THE SENSORY WORLD OF THE WOMB

Understanding the sensory input your baby was used to in the womb, will help you make her transition to the outside world – and the period of maturation of her sensory system – smooth and happy. Let's take a look at Amy's comfortable sensory environment in the womb.

Touch and proprioception

Amy's sense of touch is the first sense to begin to develop when she is an embryo of only three weeks. By 12 weeks her entire body is sensitive to touch, except the top of her head, which remains insensitive throughout her development in the womb, probably because of the impending big squeeze through the birth canal.

The temperature is always perfect – a temperature we call neutral warmth. There is no light touch in the womb – only deep pressure touch. The elastic uterus provides Amy with constant deep pressure, like an all-day hug or massage. As Amy moves against resistance in this small space, she receives a lot of feedback from her muscles about her body's position.

Hearing

Amy's sense of hearing is fully developed by 28 weeks and on the day she's born she has about 12 weeks' listening experience. So what is Amy hearing whilst she is in the womb? All sounds are muted and reach Amy's ears through water, making the sound waves slow down. She therefore receives sounds at a lower frequency. Even when the world outside is silent, Amy hears the quiet gushes of amniotic fluid and blood flowing in the veins and of course Mom's heartbeat and digestion. These background noises contribute to the constant white noise she hears.

Sight
Amy's sense of sight is her least developed sense at birth, partly because it receives very little stimulation in the womb, where light is muted and it's often quite dark, depending on what Mom's wearing. Even with direct sunlight on her mom's tummy, Amy is protected from harsh white light by her eyelids and what remains of her mom's stomach muscles.

Movement and gravity
The sense of movement and gravity from the balance (vestibular) system in the ears begins to function at five months and, like the sense of hearing and touch, is very well developed at birth. But it will only reach full maturity much later, when Amy reaches adolescence.

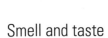

In the womb Amy is swimming in a warm pool, freely moving in a swaying bubble. As amniotic fluid decreases the effect of gravity by 50 times, Amy has the wonderful sensation of being as light as a feather – only two per cent of the weight she would feel outside the womb.

Amy feels most movements as rocking in one or other direction, so she is constantly rocked to sleep. Whenever her mom rests or lies down, the lulling movement stops and she may become wakeful and busy. During the third trimester, Amy's vestibular system has matured sufficiently for her to sense gravity and turn to the appropriate head down position in preparation for birth. In this head down position, Amy's vestibular system is strongly stimulated, which is important for her developing muscle tone.

Smell and taste
Amy's senses of smell and taste begin to function at 28 weeks. By the last trimester they are so highly tuned that Amy can taste the food her mom eats and even smell odours from the outside world. Even in the womb Amy prefers sweet tastes.

By the last trimester, much of Amy's sensory system is quite well developed, getting ready to deal with the outside world. So Amy lives in an incredibly stimulus-rich environment and is appropriately stimulated in the womb. She hears the gurgles, squeaks, throbs and gushes of her mom's body and she feels the vibrations of her mom's movements, voice and heartbeat. She can taste the flavour and feel the warmth of the amniotic fluid. Amy perceives her own movements within the relatively gravity-free environment, the pressure of the walls of the uterus against her, as well as the sensory input from her own developing organs.

Although there appears to be a barrage of sensory input, most of this input is calming stimuli. So Amy begins life in a wonderfully calming world – the ideal place from a sensory perspective and for most babies, a place where they are most comfortable.

CHAPTER 2

How sensory input affects your baby's state

As Jack emerges from the womb, he begins to splutter and then lets out a wail. He cries and his arms wave uncontrollably as he searches the room with his eyes, taking in the very foreign, blurry space. Sensing his disorganisation, his mom wraps his arms to his chest and brings him towards her. His eyes find hers and he settles and becomes focused intently on Mom and Dad. In this magic, calm-alert state, Mom, Dad and Babe explore each other's faces. Jack settles and remains in a calm-alert state for over an hour before beginning to fuss and squirm. Mom cuddles him close to her and he falls asleep. Only two hours old, Jack is processing his sensory world and has experienced the crying, calm and sleep states.

SENSORY INPUT

From the moment of birth, your baby begins to perceive sensory information. Even the calmest labour room is full of new sensory experiences.

Sight

At birth, Jack can see a fuzzy picture of the world. He focuses best on objects that are about 20 cm away – the perfect distance to make out his mom's features when he is lying in her arms or feeding at her breast.
Initially he sees high contrast or black-and-white images most clearly. By the end of his first week, he recognizes his mom's face.

Touch

At birth Jack's sense of touch is one of his most advanced abilities. Although he can't see his mom clearly, he immediately feels her calming touch when she cuddles him. He also feels the change in temperature from the warm environs of the womb to the cold air of the delivery room. He'll feel the painful prick of a needle, but it will be a while before his sense of touch is advanced enough for him to know exactly where he is being touched or pricked.

As Jack is touched and moves his body, his brain begins to form an internal map of his body. This awareness is vital for the development of motor and perceptual skills later. It's hard to imagine, but regular gentle massage when Jack is

Emotional development is closely linked to the sense of touch. Positive touch experiences such as massage, swaddling and cuddles release 'happy hormones' called endorphins in the brain, which condition your baby for positive emotional responses to interactions.

a baby could have an impact on his skipping skills and even his maths ability in Grade 2! Furthermore, touch also plays a vital role in Jack's **emotional development** and how he feels.

Hearing

After birth Jack hears completely different sounds from those he heard in the womb because the amniotic fluid no longer mutes and slows down sound. Every noise he hears sounds louder and harsher. His mom's voice is a firm favourite as it is the clearest voice he heard in the womb and the one he is most likely to recognize.

During the first year Jack will channel energy into first determining where sounds are coming from and later making sense of the sounds he hears. Loud and irregular sounds are distressing or alerting, whilst quiet, rhythmical white noise will help calm him down.

Movement and gravity

Once Jack is born, his movement or vestibular system is suddenly confronted with his body feeling 50 times heavier than before, and having to move against gravity. The greatest motor goal of the first year is to gain control against gravity. The sense of movement is absolutely vital for the development of Jack's motor skills, such as being able to roll and later crawl around on the floor. The normal progression of all his other movements is based upon his vestibular system.

Smell and taste

Jack's sense of smell is so sensitive at birth that he can soon identify the smell of his own mother's breast milk on a cotton swab. If his mother is his principle care-giver (especially if he is breast-fed), Jack will soon know and recognize his mother's smell better than his father's. Jack prefers sweet tastes, which may explain why breast milk is so sweet. Sweet tastes also help Jack stay in an optimal state for interaction, and encourage him to move his hands to his mouth – a very important self-calming strategy.

SENSE-ABLE SECRET Since smells elicit emotions faster than any other sense, it is vital to keep your baby's world of smell calming.

YOUR BABY'S STATES

To understand the effect of sensory input on your baby, we should look at the states through which he moves in a day. Jack spends part of each day sleeping and part awake. These are two very clear states. But within each of these two states are other identifiable states.

Sleep states

When Jack's mom checks on him while he is sleeping, she notices that sometimes he's in a light sleep where his eyelids flutter and he stirs quite easily. If the doorbell rings when Jack is in this state, he is likely to wake up. At other times he sleeps so soundly that she holds her breath and leans close to Jack to hear if he is breathing. These two states of sleep are **Light Sleep** or Rapid Eye Movement sleep and **Deep Sleep** or non-Rapid Eye Movement sleep.

Wakeful states

Jack has many wakeful states. In the **Drowsy** state just before or just after sleep his eyes look heavy and he displays a 'thousand-yard stare' – looking into the distance, not focusing on much at all. As he wakes up further he enters a very responsive and content state. We call this the **Calm-Alert** state. In this wakeful state Jack is focused and really enjoys interaction. He has attentive expressions, displays minimal movement and is focused on specific stimulation. This is the state in which Jack responds best to his world, and is most likely to learn and benefit from interaction. If he becomes very stimulated whilst in this state, he enters the **Active-Alert** state where he kicks and moves his body excitedly and very vigorously. This is not the best state for learning as Jack receives too much input from his busily moving muscles. This movement stimulation interferes with learning and distracts him. In this state he also runs the risk of sensory overload. Jack's mom notes that once he is in this state, it's not long before he begins to fuss and may even enter the **Crying** state.

The effect of sensory input on these states

Picture Jack's states in ascending order, with Crying at the top and Deep Sleep at the bottom. Now let's see how sensory input affects these states.

Stimulatory, alerting or distressing input will generally move Jack up a state. A loud noise (stimulatory) can move him from Deep Sleep to Light Sleep or even wake him from Light Sleep. In the same way seeing a new face may move Jack from a Drowsy state into a Calm-Alert state. But too many faces may stimulate him so much that he goes from the Calm-Alert through the Active-Alert state to Crying.

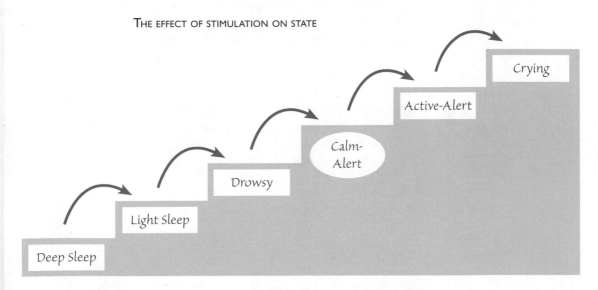

THE EFFECT OF STIMULATION ON STATE

Conversely, **calming input** tends to move Jack's state down a level. If his nervous system is calmed, his state calms down too. Soft music can make a Drowsy Jack fall asleep and even cause him to move quickly into Deep Sleep. Gentle rocking can soothe him when he's in the Crying state, making him more ready for inter-action (Calm-Alert state) or sleep.

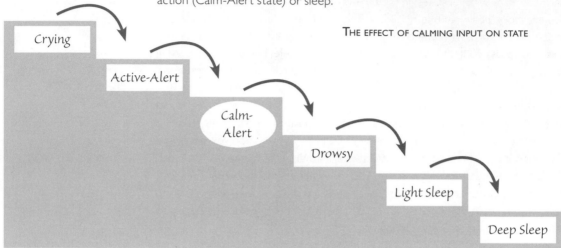

THE EFFECT OF CALMING INPUT ON STATE

CALMING VS ALERTING SENSORY INPUT

In our everyday world certain substances, such as caffeine, are stimulants; others, such as tranquillizers, calm us down. The same holds true for the sensory world: some sensory input is calming and other alerting or even distressing. Rough handling or jarring noises make you feel on edge, but few things are more relaxing than the calming smells and the deep touch of a massage.

The womb is an ideal calming environment. If you understand this environ-ment, you can recreate it when appropriate to calm your baby, especially during the early weeks, when the transition from womb to busy sensory world is the most drastic. Regulating your baby's sensory environment in the first few weeks and months can make this transition smoother and positively affect many facets of his development.

Understanding what input can be used to calm your baby and what should be avoided, especially if he is already over-stimulated, is invaluable so you can settle him when he is fussing and help him regulate his states. Use the following quick-glance table to help you structure a calm world for your baby.

SENSE	CALMING	HOW?	ALERTING	HOW?
TOUCH	Deep touch pressure Touch to the back Neutral warmth Smooth & soft textures Touch in and around the mouth	• Handle firmly • Deep hugs • Cover with blankets • Food or environment • Initially use smooth textures of food • Soft bedding & clothing • Hands to mouth • Sucking	Light touch Unpredictable touch Touch on the front of the body & face Extreme temperatures Mixed textures	• Tickling • Blowing • Touch without warning • Food or environment • Lumpy or coarse food • Scratchy carpet, blanket or clothing
SENSE OF BODY POSITION	Sustained positions Resisted movements	• Holding baby • Swaddle	Changes in body position Quick movements of limbs	• Rough play – in older baby
MOVEMENT	Slow, rhythmical linear movements	• Rocking • Swaying • Carrying in pouch • Rocking chair	Fast, irregular movements Angular or spinning	• Swinging through the air – in older baby
SMELL	Neutral smells Smells associated with positive experiences	• Lavender, camomile • Mother smell • Baby smell	Strong, pungent smells	• Perfume • Tobacco or smoke • Chemicals • Detergents • Citrus, cinnamon
SIGHT	Muted light Calming, natural colours	• Light dimmer • Natural light • Block-out curtains • Pale colours & teal blue	Bright light Bright, contrasting colours	• Fluorescent light • Flashing lights • Red, cerise
HEARING	White noise Familiar sounds Rhythmic sounds Low pitch	• Static • Background noise • Heartbeat • Lullabies • Baroque/classical music • Crooning or humming	Unpredictable noises High or fluctuating pitch Loud noises	• Excited or anxious voices • Screaming & shouting
TASTE	Familiar, mild tastes Sweet tastes	• Milk	Strong tastes	• Sour, bitter or salty • Citrus

Regulating your baby's state

The important skill of regulating your state develops with maturity. By adulthood, most of us have acquired this skill, so we can fall asleep without being rocked or massaged and we don't throw temper tantrums or burst into tears when things don't go our way. An older baby or toddler who manages to fall asleep with ease or get through a party without a temper tantrum, shows that he has learnt to regulate his state by not becoming over-stimulated and is able to move from a drowsy state to a sleep state without needing help. This self-regulation develops over time. You will help your baby develop self regulation by understanding his different states and how sensory information affects these states.

- The Calm-Alert state is a precious state for **learning**. At birth your baby will have very short Calm-Alert periods as he needs so much sleep and is easily over-stimulated when awake. But as each day passes, the time he spends in the Calm-Alert state increases, allowing more time for controlled stimulation and interaction. By six months old he will cope with being awake for two hours and will probably spend 45 to 60 minutes of that time happily learning from his world in the Calm-Alert state.

- Every baby's capacity to filter stimulation is **unique** – while one baby can remain in the Calm-Alert state for a long time, even when there is a lot going on, another baby may become over-stimulated at the drop of a hat. This explains why Jack remains a happy baby for most of a busy family lunch, while his cousin Evan fusses every time he is greeted by a new face or is stimulated in any way.

- Clearly since the optimal state for learning is the Calm-Alert state, you should try to **help your baby** maintain this state when he is awake. That way your baby will interact optimally with the environment, remaining calm but initiating stimulation during these periods.
  - Use *calming* input to settle your baby's state when he becomes fractious.
  - Regular *day sleeps* help renew his ability to self-regulate and remain calm.
  - *Quiet spaces* to have 'quiet time' are important for your little one to help him regulate his state.
  - From around three months of age, you can teach your baby to *self-soothe* to shift down a state from Active Alert to Calm Alert by finding his own self-soothing tool, such as sucking his fingers or using a comfort blanket.

- Once you have determined your baby's threshold for stimulation, you will find it easy to help him **regulate his state**. Regulating his state will help to get your baby to sleep. When working on a flexible schedule, you will know approximately when your baby will be tired and you can use appropriate sensory input to calm him down before bedtime (see sensory input table on page 19).

- There will be **times in your baby's life** when regulation may become more of a challenge. When he is dealing with stress in any way such as teething, illness or a new and overwhelming environment, your baby may regress and find it difficult to stay calm. This is part of life no matter how old you are.

- Along your journey into parenthood you will learn which stimuli will calm your baby and which will excite him.

At six weeks of age Jack was baptized. During the day he was bombarded with sensory stimuli from family and friends and by the end of the day he was over-stimulated and very tired. As he began to fuss, his mother recognized the signs and used calming strategies. She removed him from the bright, noisy environment and took him to a room with drawn curtains. She swaddled him tightly and placed him in a sling for deep pressure touch, neutral warmth, rocking motion and her familiar smell. Once Jack was calm, she removed him from the sling, keeping him swaddled, and placed him gently between pillows on the bed to contain him. She gave him his hands to suck and hummed a monotonous low-toned lullaby as Jack drifted off to sleep.

CHAPTER 3

Preparing your baby's sensory environment

Cathy is making the final preparations for her baby's arrival. The thought of leaning over the cot and gazing at its tiny new occupant, probably too small for even newborn-size baby clothes, fills her with excitement (and, if she's honest, a touch of trepidation). As she busily prepares, she wonders if she should choose blue or pink curtains for her baby's room and considers which style of décor is least likely to date. Her husband, Pete, on the other hand just wonders how much this nursery decoration and all these baby clothes are going to cost!

But it's not just what you can afford or what is in vogue that should dictate how you decorate the nursery and what pre-birth plans should be made. By now you have seen how sensory input can affect a baby's mood and behaviour, so it stands to reason that you should also consider the sensory implications of the choices you make when preparing your baby's environment. Since the womb is the ideal calming environment, you should try to recreate that environment when appropriate over the next few weeks and months. This will help ensure a smooth, happy transition from the womb to the world, which will have a positive effect on many facets of your baby's development. In a nutshell, you should prepare a calm room and surround your baby with soothing sensory input for the first months, if she is going to be the calm and content baby you desire.

THE NURSERY

Most parents prepare a special room or nursery for their baby. But whether their baby sleeps in that room from the beginning or shares her parent's room or bed initially, is variable. Sometimes a baby must share a room with her parents because there simply is no other room.

Sometimes parents prefer to have their baby sleeping in their room, especially if either parent suffers from anxiety over separation or loss. Yet another mom may find that she gets no sleep with all the noisy grunts a sleeping baby makes. Many parents have their baby in their bedroom for at least the first few days.

Since there is no right or wrong, it is important to listen to your instincts and do what works for you in your particular situation. With a view to ensuring good sleeping habits in the long term, if space permits and you are comfortable to do so, aim to have your baby in her own room by three months of age. At this stage, the transition to her own sleep space is straightforward because she has not developed sleep expectations.

Babies are very noisy sleepers and your child may keep you awake when you should be sleeping to be rested for the next night feed. Furthermore, when your baby is in the Light Sleep part of a sleep cycle, she will be more likely to wake if you are moving about in your room.

To establish good sleeping habits from the outset, it is vital in these early months that you provide the best environment possible for your baby to be able to sleep peacefully for long stretches. Regardless of where your baby sleeps, follow two key principles:

- Her sleep zone must be **calm and conducive to sleep**. This space should not be an area that your baby will associate with play or feeding, rather a space that is calm and peaceful.
- Her sleep zone must be **consistent**. This is particularly true from three months onwards when she will begin to associate a certain space with sleep. Try to consistently get her to sleep for at least one day sleep and for bedtime in her sleep zone.

Touch

Bed linen must be soft because rough textures are more likely to wake your baby at night. Stretch cotton cot sheets are wonderful. Receiving blankets, soft sarongs, and pure sheepskins make excellent bottom sheets. Receiving blankets that have a bit of stretch in them are essential for **swaddling**, which is very important in the early days. Swaddling is the best way for us to imitate the tight hug of the womb environment. It provides deep-touch pressure and also prevents your baby's little limbs from shooting out in a startle reflex – a common cause of night wakings in young babies. When you swaddle your baby, ensure her hands are near her face for self-soothing.

You can also buy or make a **happy hugger**: a fabric-covered beanbag filled with safe and hypo-allergenic material that can be gently warmed in the microwave. These are available in many shapes, and are even found in the shape of a hand or an animal. Put a drop of lavender oil on the fabric to make it even more calming. When placed on your baby or next to her, a happy hugger is wonderfully calming and soothing, providing deep-touch pressure and neutral warmth.

CAUTION	Do not overheat the happy hugger since a small baby cannot move away from the heat source.

Smell

Drops of lavender oil on linen or in a burner in the room are calming and will help your baby sleep well. You can also put an item of clothing that smells of Mom (not her perfume) in the cot for comfort.

Sight

A light with a **dimmer** is an essential for night feeds. Keep the night feed environment as calm, dark and quiet as possible to ensure that your baby goes back to

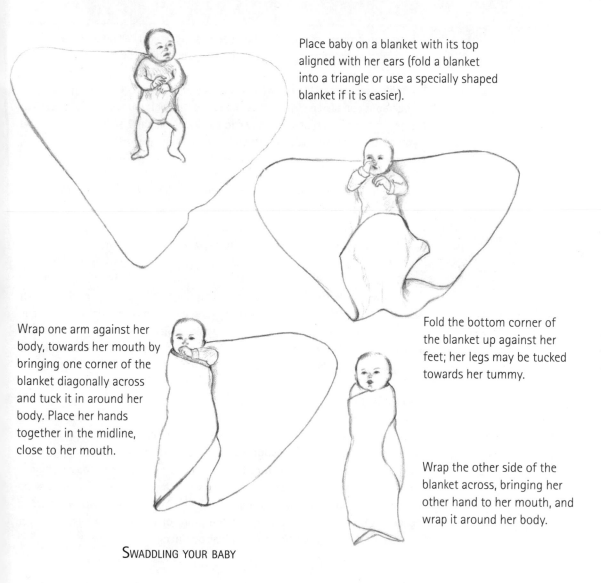

Place baby on a blanket with its top aligned with her ears (fold a blanket into a triangle or use a specially shaped blanket if it is easier).

Wrap one arm against her body, towards her mouth by bringing one corner of the blanket diagonally across and tuck it in around her body. Place her hands together in the midline, close to her mouth.

Fold the bottom corner of the blanket up against her feet; her legs may be tucked towards her tummy.

Wrap the other side of the blanket across, bringing her other hand to her mouth, and wrap it around her body.

SWADDLING YOUR BABY

sleep after the feed. If the room is fully lit and you speak to or play with your baby, she may think it's daytime again so she can play for the next hour (which you won't enjoy at 2 am).

For the first few months, decorate the room in **muted colours** with few contrasts. Good colours are neutrals, as well as the traditional baby hues of pale yellow, blue, pink and green. If you like bright colours, wait until your baby is six months old before decorating the room in a bright trendy fabric or colourful gingham check.

Curtains with **block-out lining** will make the room darker and more womb-like, to promote calm sleep times. This is especially important for daytime sleep periods, which your baby will need right up to three years old. An overtired baby does not sleep well at night, so daytime sleeps are important from the outset.

From about three months your baby begins to connect falling asleep with specific associations. If she comes to associate falling asleep with being rocked, she will expect to be rocked to sleep at all night wakings. This may not be a problem in the early days, but as your baby gets older, sleep associations can become habits that disturb both your and your baby's sleep. Sleep associations that your baby can use independently, such as hand-to-mouth or a security blanket, should be encouraged (see page 48).

Do not put any **toys or mobiles** in or near the cot. The cot must be a calm sleeping space only, not a stimulating play area. To encourage eye focus, keep a few contrasting colour toys or pictures (red, black and white) near the changing mat where it is appropriate for your baby to be awake and stimulated.

Hearing

To help your baby fall asleep and to facilitate unbroken periods of sleep, refer back to the world of the womb. White noise and womb sounds are calming in the early weeks. Buy or make a CD of **white noise** by recording the vacuum cleaner or radio static. Also available are CDs of **calming music** 'mixed' with the steady beating of a heart, lullabies or baroque music compilations for babies.

Movement

A rocking chair is useful for feed times. Ensure it is comfortable and provides support for your arms and neck – you'll be spending a lot of time in it in the early days. Your baby will love the **soothing, rocking motion**. Don't use it to get your baby to actually fall asleep, but rather to calm her into a Drowsy state before sleep time. Some people buy rocking cribs, which are also nice for baby to sleep in, as they provide that little extra calming input. You can buy a voice-activated vibrating gadget which is attached to the pram or cot and vibrates whenever your baby cries. The vibrating motion is also calming.

CLOTHING

Buying and receiving gifts of those first tiny baby outfits is so exciting. But some of the more elaborate and appealing clothes will not be comfortable for your baby's new, sensitive skin. A piece of lace around the neck or the denim fabric of those cute baby dungarees may irritate your baby and contribute to her fussing at certain times of the day. Your baby may not indicate immediately how irritated she is getting but later, the usual irritable hour in the evening may be worse than usual because of the accumulation of this sensory input.

Touch

Clothing may cause frequent wakings if the fabric is rough or the seams prickly. Use **soft fabrics** and even turn vests inside out if the seams disturb your baby.

Denim, corduroy, lace, stiff cotton, scratchy wool and other stiff or scratchy fabrics can be irritating for your baby.

Smell

Detergents leave a smell on your baby's clothes. Even the lightest fragrance that we barely notice is pungent to your new baby's sensitive sense of smell. Some fragrances and chemicals are irritants to a newborn's skin and can even cause allergies. Therefore, the products you use to wash and rinse your baby's clothes may have an impact on her state. For the first six weeks use fragrance-free baby washing powder and add a tablespoon (15 ml) of vinegar to the final rinsing water instead of softener. Vinegar is an effective, fragrance-free softener.

MOTHER SPACE

When your baby first leaves the womb, she will spend most of her waking hours in 'mother space' – the first space your baby enters after being born, where she will be happiest for many months to come. We call this 'mother space', even though it also applies to dads and other primary caregivers. For the first few months this space has a major impact on your baby. So follow the principles of a calm environment outlined above with regard to your clothes and the space around you when your baby is with you.

Smell

Try not to wash your baby immediately after birth. Only wash the vernix off after a few days. This white, waxy covering is clean and good for the skin. Babies are familiar with the smell of amniotic fluid and **vernix**. There is even evidence that an unwashed baby is more likely to bring her hands to her mouth sooner after birth than washed babies. Hand-to-mouth is one of the first really clever and important strategies your baby will use to self-calm and one that will make your life much easier.

Besides vernix, the soothing smells of mother space are the best calming input at this stage. So hold your baby or have her near you as much as possible in the early days. Don't wear any perfume, deodorant or after-shave lotion until your baby is much older and even then only introduce smells slowly and watch your baby's reactions. The **fragrance** of perfume and after-shave lotion can easily overload your baby, especially true if you're breast-feeding since your baby will be physically very close to you. Dad should try to remove his work clothes as soon as he comes home. This cuts out all the smells carried on work clothes, to which your baby could be extremely sensitive.

Sight

Wear a little **make-up**, especially around your eyes, to draw attention to your face. This helps improve your baby's focus and early interaction. As a secondary benefit, you may find that wearing a bit of make-up will raise your morale at a time in your life when you feel much more functional than pretty! Another way to feel better and to attract your baby's attention is by smiling. It also serves to reinforce socialization.

Touch

In the womb, your baby feels the consistent, deep pressure, skin-to-skin contact of the uterus. Try to apply these principles in the early days. All babies, especially premature babies (who have not benefitted from a full nine months in the womb) and those born by Caesarean section (without the tight touch pressure of the birth canal), benefit immensely from being skin to skin with their mom or dad for the few days after birth. Place your baby naked, wearing only a nappy, on your naked chest and cover you both to keep warm. This soothing space has many benefits and keeps your baby calm.

CHOOSING A BABY CARRIER

There are two main types of carrier: the upright pouch and the sling in which the baby lies almost horizontally. The sling is the best type for a young baby as her neck and body are fully supported. Your baby can even feed from this position. Some slings can also be used as an upright carrier for babies up to three years of age.

Use a **pouch** only once your baby has a degree of head control (at around four weeks). They are useful well into the ninth month and even later if your baby is small. You can face your baby inwards or outwards, depending on how much visual stimulation you want her to have at that time. If it is sleep time face her towards your chest. If she should be awake and stimulated, turn her to face outwards.

When **handling** your baby, use gentle but firm touch, making her feel secure and comforted. Wear soft, comfortable clothing that she can snuggle into. Newborns are easily over-stimulated by being handled too much and passed around. Let close family members handle her in a quiet environment when she is content, but discourage passing her around at social gatherings. Each time she is held by a new person, her sensory system takes in all the new sensory information about that person, especially the person's smell, touch and sounds.

Movement

The calming movements of rocking and swaying, similar to those experienced in the womb, are soothing for your baby. When she is awake, especially if unsettled, sway gently as you hold her. Research has shown that we naturally sway and bop our babies at a pace similar to a heartbeat (72 beats per minute). Many moms find that slow backwards-and-forwards rocking – at the same pace you would walk at – is more calming for the baby than side-to-side rocking. Use whichever movement works for you.

Compared to many other cultures, our young babies spend a lot of time away from the comfort of our bodies, in prams. When prams were invented the 'wealthy' used them so they became the vogue and a status symbol. Thereafter Western moms were told, "if you carry your baby too much you will spoil her". Over the last hundred years, these two erroneous messages (status and spoiling) have resulted in prams becoming the most common way of transporting babies. There are many good reasons why **carrying** your baby is better:

- Babies worn in slings or pouches are calmer.
- These babies sleep better at night due to the movement of the day.
- Your baby will see the world at your level and you will communicate more about what she is seeing so she will learn more.
- Babies who are carried also learn to socialise as they see their parent's response to people and have more eye contact with Mom and others.
- You can get on with various tasks without getting tense with frustration because you have to pat or rock your baby while urgent chores pile up.

INTRODUCING YOUR BABY TO THE WORLD

The day you take your baby home and introduce her to the world brings a sensory assault on all levels that is comparable only to the sensory shock of birth. Unfamiliar with the smells, sights and touches of the outside world and its people, she may have a few rocky days ahead of her. One of your first protective duties is to make this introduction to the world a smooth one. You can do this on two levels. First, by regulating her environment as discussed. Then, by limiting the amount of unfamiliar handling she receives in the early days, you will help to keep her calm and happy.

Limit the number of **visitors** initially. Both you and your baby need your rest. You should take every opportunity to sleep when your baby does and you will also need whatever free time you get (short-lived as it may be) to prepare for the next feed and take care of yourself and the other members of your family.

Encourage a consistent sleep routine from early on, and keep your **outings** within your baby's awake time. This way her awake time is spent playing and developing, while she spends her sleep time in the early days in a quiet environment. Wherever you take your baby, the sensory input from the environment will affect her state.

The homes of friends and family are great destinations as you can also relax and usually find a quiet space to retreat to, if needed. A busy shopping centre can be very over-stimulating for your new baby. As a rule of thumb, if there are fluorescent or neon lights and busy crowds, cover the front of the pram or baby seat with a towelling nappy or cotton blanket to mute the sound, the light and other visual stimuli. If you are using a baby pouch, carry your baby facing inwards.

ESTABLISHING A 'SENSE-ABLE' ROUTINE

A newborn baby needs an inordinate amount of sleep, and in the early days (about the first two to three weeks) will sleep almost around the clock when not feeding. But it won't be long before your little angel starts to wake up to the world. Suddenly getting her to sleep at all may seem impossible. As she starts to take in the world around her, she becomes more alert. Her immature brain is not yet very good at processing the stimuli she is subjected to, which may be excessive at times. This may cause her to become fussy, irritable and sleepless – a far cry from the sleepyhead of the first two weeks.

The answer is to guide her into a flexible routine. A flexible routine built around her sleep and awake cycles within a structured environment will help keep her calm and content.

Having some structure will also help you to act confidently with regard to all aspects of your baby's care.
- It will help prevent your baby from becoming over-stimulated.
- It will prevent her from becoming hungry or over-tired.
- It will give your baby a sense of security.
- It allows you predictable time to do household chores or to relax.
- It will help you to correctly interpret your baby's moods and cries.

Guidelines for a manageable routine

By structuring your baby's environment around her needs, you can create the perfect background for a routine that is structured, but that retains some flexibility. This way you will be able to identify and meet her needs as they change.
- Set yourself attainable goals and be realistic about your role as a parent.
- Accept that you will have 'bad days' with your baby from time to time.
- Pace daily household chores around your baby's sleep and feed times and

try not to worry if unimportant household tasks take a back seat for a while. Even better is to try to delegate household chores for the first few weeks.
- Accept that you will have to plan your life around your baby's needs. Don't try to plan her routine around yours – she will win!
- Limit feed times to a maximum of 40 minutes, which includes time for bringing up winds.
- Limit your baby's awake times according to age-appropriate levels (see page 48).
- Plan care-giving, outings and activities to fall within her awake time.

SAFETY

From birth to approximately nine months your baby should be transported in a removable baby seat whilst in the car. These seats allow safe transportation and convenient carrying of babies weighing up to 9 kg. Always use a baby seat for safety when travelling, but when you arrive at your destination, take your baby out of the seat and lay her on the floor on a mat or on your lap for some exercise if it is her awake time.

From nine months onwards your baby will probably be ready for a proper car seat. These are not easily removed but provide safety during journeys.

CHAPTER 4

How your baby signals sensory load

In the womb all Mark's basic needs were met – food was delivered straight to him and he was lulled to sleep in a warm and contained environment. In the outside world Mark has to communicate with his caregivers to have his needs met. At first his parents don't understand his 'language'. But the start of this new relationship between Mark and his parents is not very different from the time, years before, when his mom and dad met. First there was that subtle locking of eyes across the room. Then in the following weeks they began to know the meaning of raised eyebrows and smiles in the eyes. Every now and then they misunderstood each other's body language and tension would erupt for a while. Now all Mark's mom has to do is rub her ear lobe for his dad to know that he's overstepped the line.

The first few weeks with Mark will be similar, as his parents learn to interpret his subtle baby talk. If they don't take the time to get to know his language, or they react before making sure they understand him, Mark will feel frustrated. If his rudimentary attempts at communication are not interpreted correctly or acknowledged, he may have to use more direct signals such as crying.

Subtle baby talk is the precious, first social interaction between you and your baby. If you listen and take note, you tell him he's important and that you respect him and value his input. Like the special looks shared between a couple newly in love, the magic of the early parent-baby relationship precedes years of love. If you start this relationship with a sensitive approach, trying to understand him and meet his needs appropriately, you will be well rewarded.

In this chapter, we explore the signals your baby uses to communicate his needs. Recognizing and understanding these signals will help you care more effectively for him and avoid periods of unnecessary crying.

UNDERSTANDING YOUR BABY'S SIGNALS

Your baby's sensory world changes the instant he is born. His behaviour when he is exposed to sensory input varies, depending on how his nervous system (brain) interprets the input. All his senses (hearing, sight, touch, smell, taste and the body senses) work together to form a complete picture of what is going on around him. **Sensory integration** is the term used to describe the critical function of the brain responsible for producing this complete picture. It is the process whereby sensory input is perceived and processed and a response is generated. For most of us, effective sensory integration occurs automatically, unconsciously and effortlessly.

Your baby's immature nervous system responds to the world either with enjoyment and appropriate interaction to the stimulation, or, when exposed to **excessive or distressing sensory stimuli**, by becoming overwhelmed by it, resulting in a fussy and irritable baby.

Unlike adults who can remove themselves from a stimulus, your baby, unable to control his world for himself, must communicate his reaction to the stimulus or event. Your baby has a language all of his own to let you know exactly how he is dealing with and responding to the sensory input from the world around him. Your baby will respond to stimuli in one of four ways (related to the states described on page 16). He may be happy and want interaction, he may start to be overwhelmed and appeal for help, he may start fussing, or he may eventually cry. He uses subtle baby talk to communicate his response to you.

Approach signals – "play with me"

When Mark is ten weeks old his parents take him along to a dinner. It is his first major social event and his dad feels very proud as his little boy interacts with friends and family by cooing and even showing off his new smile. At this point, early on in the evening, Mark is ready for social interaction and shows many signs that he is 'happy and ready'.

When your baby interprets stimuli as non-stressful and responds to the stimuli appropriately, he displays Approach signals. These signals indicate to you that he is neurologically well-organized, content and ready to interact with the world. Your baby is now in the Calm-Alert state.

Calm-Alert   Approach signals

- Smiling, or mouthing with an 'ooh' expression. A young baby (under six weeks) also 'smiles', not with his lips necessarily but with bright eyes, relaxed eyebrows, and smooth breathing.
- Soft, relaxed, but alert facial expression, with open eyes. Your baby makes eye-contact and stares into your eyes.
- Cooing.
- Relaxed limbs with smooth body movements, minimal large movements.
- Turning toward sounds.

RESPONSE

Your baby is in effect inviting you to 'Approach' him and interact. His signals say he is 'happy and ready'. While your baby is in the Calm-Alert state and inviting interaction, you should make eye-contact with him, stimulate, talk to and play with him.

Warning signals – "help me"

A little later that same evening, having been stimulated by this new environment, Mark has moved from the Calm-Alert state into the Active-Alert state. He is starting to feel a little overwhelmed and uncomfortable and now gives Warning signals and self-help signals showing that he is trying to stop himself from becoming over-stressed by the excessive stimulation.

When your baby starts feeling a little stressed by all the input from his world, he starts to behave in a manner that will help him decrease the effect of that stress. He does this in an attempt to help himself stay calm. Your baby's signals must now be interpreted as Warning signals that he may be reaching overload. He still has the ability to self-organize and regulate his state at this point, but this is established at some cost and takes a lot of effort.

Active-Alert		Warning signals

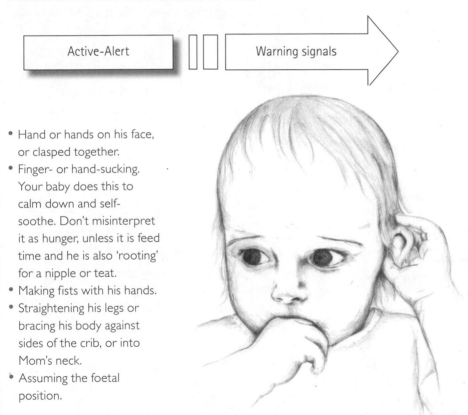

- Hand or hands on his face, or clasped together.
- Finger- or hand-sucking. Your baby does this to calm down and self-soothe. Don't misinterpret it as hunger, unless it is feed time and he is also 'rooting' for a nipple or teat.
- Making fists with his hands.
- Straightening his legs or bracing his body against sides of the crib, or into Mom's neck.
- Assuming the foetal position.

Your baby is giving Warning signals, indicating that he is feeling uncomfortable, but is trying hard to self-calm. If the exposure to the stimuli continues, his nervous system will be pushed into overload and he will start fussing. Avoid any further stimulation, remove him from the stimulating environment and allow your baby to go to sleep if he needs to.

Fussing signals — "Back off"

Unfortunately Mark's mom does not pick up on his subtle Warning signals, so it's not long before Mark becomes over-stimulated by all the noise, smells and touches associated with the outing. By now he is no longer able to self-calm and begins to fuss. These are clear signs that Mark is not happy and needs a change of environment. If Mark could talk, he would simply tell you, "Take me from all this input or let me be alone".

If your baby is not removed from the stimulating environment or helped to calm himself or sleep, he will become **over-stimulated**. At this point he is so stressed by the stimulation that he is unable to overcome the effect of the sensory input by self-calming. The input has simply exceeded his ability to cope and the stability of his nervous system is compromised. This period is characterized by fussing, but your baby may not actually be crying yet. These signs are often misinterpreted as digestive disturbances (colic), boredom or are even missed altogether.

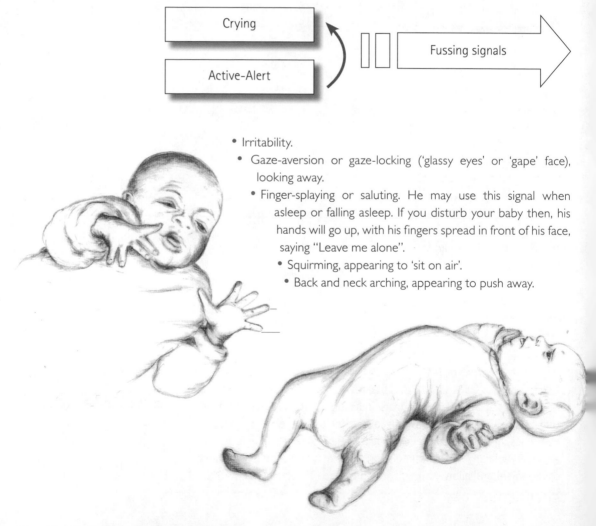

- Irritability.
- Gaze-aversion or gaze-locking ('glassy eyes' or 'gape' face), looking away.
- Finger-splaying or saluting. He may use this signal when asleep or falling asleep. If you disturb your baby then, his hands will go up, with his fingers spread in front of his face, saying "Leave me alone".
- Squirming, appearing to 'sit on air'.
- Back and neck arching, appearing to push away.

- Frantic, disorganized, jerky movements, sometimes accompanied by sweaty feet, especially when he becomes over-stimulated by a mobile or other visual stimulation.
- Tongue thrusting.
- Grimacing, frowning and grunting.
- Yawning, sneezing, hiccups. Your baby may be yawning from tiredness if it is sleep time, or sneezing to clear his nose, or indeed have hiccups after a feed, BUT before immediately assuming this is so, look at the circumstances and timing.
- Colour changes such as paleness, mottling, flushing and a bluish discolouration around the mouth (frequently attributed to winds or gas). Such colour changes can be a nervous system response to fatigue or sensory overload.
- Changes in vital signs such as heart rate and/or respiration, for example panting, with irregular breaths.
- Gagging, spitting-up.

RESPONSE

When your baby starts to fuss, give him the time out he is asking for, by removing him from the stimulus, or removing the stimulus from his environment. Very importantly, teach him how to self-calm by putting his hands to his mouth, and gently give calming input (see page 62).

Crying

Misinterpreting his signals, Mark's mother may try moving back into his line of vision when he looks away, or try to feed him when he sucks his hands to self-calm. This probably makes him feel misunderstood and limits his ability to learn to use his own special tools to self-calm (tools such as sucking his hands, curling into a ball, looking away, staring into space, and so on). Instead, Mark will become totally dependent on his mother or caregiver to calm him, and he may also be exposed to many periods of over-stimulation because his subtle cues saying "Enough is enough" are misinterpreted or missed altogether.

If your baby continues to be stimulated or is not helped to sleep when he is over-stimulated and fussing, it will not be long before he starts crying inconsolably. There is little that can undermine your confidence more and make you feel more incompetent as a parent than a crying, seemingly inconsolable baby.

> SENSE-ABLE SECRET
> Stop and take time to read and interpret your baby's signals correctly.

Mark's mom and dad learn this the hard way. Mark starts crying and continues crying so long and hard that they eventually have to leave the dinner early, leaving their (as yet childless) friends vowing never to have children of their own.

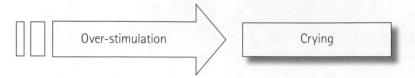

When your baby begins to cry, you will naturally look for the reason why. At times he may cry because he is hungry, ill or simply uncomfortable. In Chapter 7 – Reasons for crying (see page 56) – you will find information on how to exclude hunger or illness as a cause of crying. But what happens when you have ruled out the basics and your baby remains fractious and unsettled?

OVER-STIMULATED CRYING

When your baby starts to cry inconsolably and there is no obvious reason, in other words he is not hungry, needing a nappy change or ill, then you should consider the possibility of over-stimulation.

- Look at your baby's environment. Is it full of alerting or new sensory input? If so, it is possible that your baby has taken in too much information. His brain, being immature, is then unable to filter out or regulate the input (see page 11) and this situation could well be the cause of his crying.
- Think back to the signals he was giving just before the crying spell. If he was fussing and giving warning signals and yet continued to be stimulated, he may reach such a state of disorganization that he is unable to self-calm, and cries inconsolably.
- If your baby is constantly over-stimulated and deprived of quiet time or sleep, he will remain in this state of stress, resulting in an inability to interact happily socially. This may result in fussy feeding.
- Every baby's cry is individual and you will quickly learn to interpret your baby's over-stimulated cry. In a young baby it is accompanied by pulling up of legs, blueness around the mouth and bringing hands towards the face and mouth as he attempts to self-soothe. In an older baby, fractious niggling accompanied by tugging his ears and pushing away toys or food may indicate an over-stimulated cry.

TIREDNESS AND OVER-STIMULATION

As your baby gets fatigued, he becomes more fractious and irritable and is less able to deal with interactions and stimulation. His ability to self-soothe and display clear signals becomes less effective. When your baby is displaying warning signals he may still be able to calm himself by sucking his hands or just keeping them near his mouth or face. Once he is overtired, these self-soothing strategies are hard for him to access. Your baby's ability to be happily awake and peacefully asleep is determined by appropriate stimulations coupled with an understand-ing of his signals, but also by the duration of his awake time. Young babies have limited time periods during which they are able to be happily awake. As your baby approaches the end of that time, he should be put to sleep. But if you miss that window of opportunity (where he is tired and ready to fall asleep), he may extend into a second wind where he will appear to carry on interacting happily. However, this second wind is not without cost. Soon an over-stimulated and over-tired baby will begin to cry inconsolably. See Chapter 6, page 48 for age-appropriate guidelines for your baby's **awake** times.

Sleep is essential to prevent over stimulation for a few reasons:
- When your baby is overtired, his body produces stress hormones, such as cortisol and adrenaline in large quantities to keep him awake. This results in very busy, irritable behaviour and ultimately your baby is likely to fight sleep when it is sleep time.
- When your baby sleeps, he resets his brain's ability to cope with the next round of interaction and stimulation, so that when he wakes he is ready to be stimulated and learn from his world again.
- During periods of deep sleep, your baby's brain gets rid of the effects of over stimulation by pruning connections in the brain that are not needed.

Upon waking your baby will re-enter a calm and alert state and display approach signals again.

Over-tiredness may be the cause of crying if:
- Your baby has been awake for longer than his age-appropriate awake time (see page 48);
- He is yawning and displaying warning signals prior to beginning to fuss;
- It is early evening, and time for his night time sleep.

BODY TEMPERATURE

Young babies do not regulate their body temperature by sweating or shivering. Instead they use postures to cool down or warm up. Take note of different postures and make your baby more comfortable.

When he is cold, he is more wakeful and moves his body around more. When he is hot, he assumes the starfish position, by extending his arms and legs.

RESPONDING TO YOUR BABY'S SIGNALS	BABY'S SIGNALS	YOUR RESPONSE
	Approach signals	• Age-appropriate stimulation and interaction. (*See* Chapters 11-16.) • Talk to and play with your baby. • Interact with your baby now – this is how he will develop and learn to socialize.
	Warning signals	• Encourage self-soothing strategies to help him to self-regulate. • Don't fiddle with him too much. • Shade his eyes from glare and limit eye-contact. • Follow his lead for interactions. • Let him hold your finger if it helps him settle. • Don't automatically assume hunger or teething when you see him sucking his hands.
	Fussing signals	If you've misread his warning signals and your baby is already fussing, respond as if to warning signals and in addition: • Hold him quietly and firmly. • Regulate his environment, for example go to a quiet, non-stimulating place. • Tuck his arms in, or swaddle him in a blanket. • Play him some calming music. • Put him in a baby sling close to you. • Allow him to suck (non-nutritive).
	Crying signals	• Respond as you would to fussing signals. (*See* calming techniques on page 64 – Solutions for fussing and colic.)

CHAPTER 5

Sensory guidelines for feeding

Before Dylan was born, his mom had many preconceived ideas on all kinds of baby care issues. He wouldn't have a dummy, he would be stimulated to enhance his development, she would never have to say "no", he'd be breast-fed for a year and sleep through the night by eight weeks.

Now that Dylan is a month old, his mom realizes that no matter how many books she reads, what her parenting beliefs are or how she herself was mothered: mothering is an encounter with reality. All of her ambitious plans have been thrown out of the window as her focus shifts to the bare necessities: has Dylan had enough to eat and how long will he sleep?

The basics of baby care are feeding and sleep. In addition to love, protection and warmth, babies need proper nutrition. Obviously bodily nourishment is the primary purpose of feeding, but the vital process of parent-child bonding begins from the very first feed.

BREAST-FEEDING

Breast milk is your baby's natural food. With rare exceptions, every mother is equipped with breasts to feed her baby. Your breast milk will always suit your baby, unless you cannot breast-feed for fear of passing on the HI virus to your baby. Your health-care facility will guide and advise you about the possibility of breast-feeding your baby if you have the HI virus, but this can only be achieved after extensive counselling and under strict medical supervision.

- Exclusive breast-feeding until at least four months of age may help prevent allergies later on in life.
- Breast milk is always the right temperature and is easily digested.
- Breast-fed babies seldom have problems with constipation or diarrhoea.
- Breast milk doesn't cost anything.
- Breast milk contains maternal antibodies to boost your baby's immune system.
- Breast milk perfectly meets your baby's nutritional needs, containing just the right amounts of vitamins, minerals, protein and carbohydrates to sustain him as he grows.

The basics

Whilst breast milk is best for babies, breast-feeding does not always come naturally or easily. It is well worth investing in a good book that will guide you in the art of breast-feeding (see page 157). Since this book is not a breast-feeding manual, the topic is not covered in great detail. But here are a few guidelines for breast-feeding that might make all the difference. Appendix B on page 153 has details on expressing milk, and on weaning.

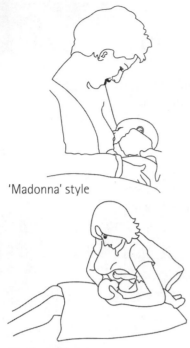

'Madonna' style

'Rugby ball' style

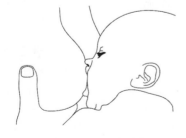

Lying down

Correct latching

- Feed your baby in a **quiet, calm environment**. Choose a comfortable chair with adequate back support and, if possible, a small stool to raise your feet off the ground. Try to **relax** before beginning. Relaxation is important for the let-down hormones which allow your milk to flow. Your baby will pick up on your calmness and feed well too.

- Take an extra minute or two to **get yourself organized** before feeding your baby. Make a cup of tea or have a glass of water or juice handy (feeding dehydrates you, so try to drink at least a cup of fluid for each feed). Put the phone on answer-mode, or keep a portable phone with you. Turn off the TV or radio and play a CD of classical or relaxation music.

- Find the most **comfortable position** in which to feed, be it the traditional 'Madonna' style of feeding with your baby lying across your tummy, or the 'rugby ball' style where you hold his body tucked safely under your arm. If you have a strong milk supply, your baby may gulp and choke on the rapid flow of milk when you feed sitting in an upright position. This can lead to excessive intake of air, which may contribute to wind and gas. In this case it is useful to lie down and allow him to feed whilst lying next to you.

- Make sure that your baby is **latched** onto the breast **correctly,** with both his top lip and his bottom lip in a snug seal around your nipple (rather like Donald Duck's 'lips' – see illustration). Ensure that both your nipple and some of the areola (dark area around the nipple) are well positioned in his mouth. If he is feeding well, his lips and jaw will compress the milk reservoirs beneath the areola, ensuring a good flow, whilst at the same time elongating your nipple to deliver the milk efficiently. Incorrect latching, with only your nipple in his mouth will cause the milk ducts in your breasts to be shut off, resulting in decreased milk flow. This will result in cracked and bruised nipples, which will be very painful for you.

- To release the suction on your breast to take your nipple out of his mouth, simply insert your finger into the corner of his mouth and gently withdraw your nipple from his mouth.

- Allow a maximum of 40 minutes per feed.

- Breast-fed babies often like to feed in 'courses' and often need a minute or two between sucks to catch their breath.

- Breast-feeding works on a supply and demand basis – the quantity of breast milk produced is directly related to how much your baby sucks. Nevertheless it can take up to six weeks to establish feeding and a milk supply. Bear this in mind when you are feeling desperate.

When problems arise with breast-feeding

Most first-time mothers would really like to give breast-feeding their best shot, and believe that this is something that comes naturally. But breast-feeding is a skill that has to be learnt – for both mom and newborn baby. Certain situations may arise in the early days that can challenge your best intentions to breast-feed. Sleep deprivation, cracked and bleeding nipples and a crying baby can all add up to a miserable and emotional mom, a stressed out dad and the idea of a pain-free feed by bottle becoming all too tempting. Let's take a look at the factors that may make breast-feeding difficult in the early days.

ENGORGED AND SWOLLEN BREASTS

If this happens, it typically occurs about four days after delivery (slightly longer after a Caesarean birth). Most new moms are usually at home by now and no longer have the support and care of the nursing staff in the maternity units to help them adjust to living with a new baby. Breasts become full and heavy, and extremely tender to touch. In some cases they become hard, hot and sore. This is what is commonly known as 'milk coming in'. It usually settles after 72 hours. Continue to feed your baby on demand, as normal, and don't be tempted to express your breasts – all you will do is encourage more milk to be produced! Place cabbage leaves in your bra (they really do work), rub arnica cream or oil onto your breasts, and take an anti-inflammatory medication to help with the pain and swelling (ask your pharmacist, clinic sister or doctor to recommend one that is safe while breast-feeding). Applying ice packs also helps ease pain and inflammation. Getting feeding right requires patience, perseverance and peaceful surroundings. It **will** get better – just give it some time. Your breasts will settle down in a few days.

MASTITIS

Mastitis is an inflammation (not necessarily an infection) of the breast. It is most commonly caused by engorged breasts and/or a blocked milk duct that has not been attended to quickly. In some cases, bacteria (*Staphylococcus aureus*) or a fungus (*Candida albicans*) from your baby's mouth or throat can enter your breasts via the nipple and cause mastitis. Blocked milk ducts commonly occur, especially in the first month of breast-feeding, when your breasts can still be swollen and sore. You can usually feel the actual spot where the blockage is, because it is sore, and if you look, you may see a red and inflamed area. It usually only occurs in one breast, and is more prevalent before a feed when your breasts are full. If feeding doesn't give you some relief and you feel as if you are coming down with flu – a bit feverish and with a headache – get help immediately!

You can also massage the area with some arnica oil or cream, and apply heat to the area after you have finished feeding. Taking anti-inflammatory medication also helps. If the mastitis is caused by a bacteria, your doctor may prescribe antibiotics. Keep a close watch on the affected area, as it may develop into a breast abscess if the blockage is not released. If the red and tender area does not lessen after a feed, and if the entire area does not settle down within a few days and you are feeling feverish and unwell, it is best to seek medical advice. You may have a breast abscess, which must be surgically drained.

If your nipples are painful, and you have shooting and burning pain during and after feeding, you may have thrush, which is caused by the *Candida albicans* fungus. Your nipples may feel itchy and tingly, and your baby may have white patches in his mouth which cannot be wiped away. You and your baby will need to be treated with specific anti-fungal medication. Ask your doctor or clinic sister for guidance.

CRACKED AND BLEEDING NIPPLES

This often leads to mothers throwing in the towel with breast-feeding because of excessive pain and discomfort with feeding. The most frequent cause of cracked nipples is incorrect latching of the baby's mouth onto the breast. Thrush can also cause very painful nipples. Make sure that your baby is latched onto the breast correctly, with both top and bottom lip in a snug seal around your nipple. Breast-feeding should not hurt and if it does it usually means that your baby has not latched correctly. To release your baby from the breast, break the suction by inserting your finger into the corner of his mouth and gently withdraw your nipple from his mouth. Then try to relatch him correctly.

Using a nipple shield (available from your pharmacy or baby shop) during feeding gives cracked and bleeding nipples time to heal. Speak to your clinic sister or doctor to recommend a nipple cream to assist with healing. Exposing your nipples to some sunlight also helps to hasten healing, but is easier said than done. Expressing breast milk and offering it to your baby from a spoon or a bottle is also a way to let your nipples heal whilst continuing to breast-feed.

EXPRESSING MILK

Breast pumps make expressing breast milk easy and will help keep up your milk supply. If you can manage to express breast milk after a feed or between feeds, this will suffice as a top-up feed, or extra feed.

NOT ENOUGH MILK

This is the most common reason mothers give for stopping breast-feeding. It is something that may occur over time due to lack of sufficient stimulation, but all women will produce enough milk for their babies, as long as the baby has full access to the breast. In the first days the volume of milk is small and highly concentrated in the form of colostrum. If a baby is offered formula feeds or given water there will be less demand on the breast, which may lead to insufficient milk if the formula feeds continue. Feeding flexibly when the baby needs it can enhance lactation. Of course rest, relaxation and a supportive environment have huge benefits for both mother and baby. It is important to weigh your baby frequently to ensure that he is growing adequately. If your baby is gaining weight, having at least six wet nappies a day, and is relatively happy between feeds (which may be very frequent in the early days, lengthening to a few hours after a few weeks), you can rest assured that you have enough milk.

Stress and anxiety, a poor diet and inadequate fluid intake may also hamper breast milk production. Make sure you are eating enough protein, such as meat, eggs and beans (you need to increase your protein intake three-fold whilst breast-feeding), drinking at least a litre of fluid a day and that feeding times are relaxed and calm. The main hormones that ensure adequate milk production are influenced by emotions, so if you are anxious and upset at feed time, these important hormones will affect your milk production and let-down.

TAKE THE GOOD DAYS WITH THE BAD:
Have realistic expectations about breast-feeding and accept that you will have both good and bad days. Initially there may seem to be more bad than good days, but follow these simple tips and hopefully breast-feeding will become easier.
- Have confidence in your ability to breast-feed.
- Gain knowledge about breast-feeding from reliable, trained sources, take time to learn and surround yourself with positive, supportive people.
- Don't ask everybody for advice – if you ask 10 people, you will get 10 different answers and be more confused. Ask women who really know and who have breast-fed their own babies.
- Latch your baby as soon as possible after birth. Ensure that your baby is correctly latched at the breast, so that the nerve impulses can travel along the correct pathways.
- Limit separation from your baby.
- Do not give your baby supplementary feeds or water in the early days.
- Let your baby lead the way – he will guide you.
- Never make your newborn baby wait for a feed.
- Eat well, sleep well and relax!
- Take time to learn.
- Breast-feeding is not supposed to hurt. It is supposed to be enjoyable for both you and baby. If breast-feeding is hurting, something is wrong. Seek assistance if this is the case.

ADVICE AT HOME
Besides professional advice, mothers are constantly being given uninitiated advice from friends and other family members. Old-fashioned recommendations, taboos, beliefs and advice not supported by clinical research are common. It is important that family members let a new mother find her own feet and it is vital that she is given encouragement and not criticism in her choices and attitude if they are different from those of other family members.

CAUTION

If you live in a rural area without access to fresh water or electricity to sterilize bottles effectively, or if you do not have the means to buy formula milk, think very carefully before stopping breast-feeding.

BOTTLE-FEEDING

If you have made the decision to start feeding your baby formula, or have been forced to do so because of medication you are taking or a return to work, today's wide choice of milk formulas enables you to ensure that your baby will be well fed. Infant formulas today are highly advanced and are available as hypo-allergenic, lactose-free, cow's milk protein-free, anti-reflux, soya bean protein feeds and pre-acidified – to name but a few! Ask your paediatrician or clinic sister to help you choose.

The basics

Follow these general guidelines for successful bottle-feeding:
- Do not give cow's milk to babies under a year as it contains too little iron and vitamins A, C and D, is difficult to digest, and is too high in protein and sodium.
- It may take a few formula changes before you find one that is best suited for your baby. There is no harm in trying different formulas, provided you do not chop and change too quickly. Try a new formula for at least 72 hours before abandoning it.
- If there is a strong history of allergies in your family, take this into careful consideration when choosing a formula.
- Always follow the manufacturer's instructions regarding preparation and mixing and ensure that the bottles and teats used are clean and sterilized.
- Hold your baby close to you, as you would if you were breast-feeding, preferably with skin-to-skin contact. Open the front of your clothing, so that he can lie close to your skin and touch your chest and neck.
- Allow a maximum of 40 minutes per feed. He may need a break half-way through, for a minute or two, to catch his breath before starting again.
- If you can hear him gulping his milk, he is most likely drinking too fast and may end up with tummy cramps caused by wind. Adjust the flow by selecting a smaller teat or adjusting the angle of the bottle. You will soon find out whether he likes to drink rapidly, or if he prefers to take his time.

How much milk does my baby need?

The general rule to calculate the amount of milk is:
150 ml milk per kilogram of baby's body weight, divided by the number of feeds you are giving in 24 hours. For example, if your baby's weight is 5 kg and you feed him six times in 24 hours:
$$5 \times 150 = 750 \text{ ml} \div 6 = 125 \text{ ml per feed}$$
This is a guideline only. Some really hungry babies demand 200 ml per kilogram of their body weight, while others may do well on 120 ml per kilogram of body weight. Let your baby guide you. If he is constantly finishing his allotted amount and still looks hungry, add a little more (try an extra 25 ml to start with) and see how he reacts. If he has had enough, he will refuse more. If he is still hungry, he will drink eagerly.

Supplementary or complementary bottle-feeding

Supplementary feeding is when a bottle of formula is given immediately after a breast-feed. This is also often called 'top up' feeding.

Complementary feeding is when a bottle of formula milk is given as a full feed on its own where breast-feeding is the norm at other feeds.

When it comes to the end of the day (or after a really bad night), you may feel that your milk supply is low. This is because the release of oxytocin, one of the milk-producing hormones, is negatively influenced by your own sensory overload and exhaustion at the end of the day. If you are very busy with demands from other children or a hectic career, you may notice it even more. The problem may be compounded if you have not taken in enough fluids and have become mildly dehydrated, by lack of rest (rest stimulates prolactin, another milk-producing hormone) or by a period of time without nipple stimulation from your baby. This may very well be the time to offer your baby a formula feed, either as a top-up, or as a full feed on its own.

THE SENSORY EXPERIENCE OF FEEDING

There are sensory implications to both breast- and bottle-feeding. Feeding is a very sensual experience, no matter how old your baby is, or how he is fed. From the moment you lift your baby into your arms and throughout the feed, each one of his senses will be stimulated.

TOUCH	The touch of your naked breast or your hands caressing him
HEARING	Your voice and the sound of your heartbeat
SIGHT	Seeing and focusing on your face and on what is around him
MOVEMENT	Being lifted into the feeding position
SMELL	The smell of your milk and 'mother space'
TASTE	Whether the milk is sweet or carries the flavour of food you ate, hot or cold
INTEROCEPTION	The inner sensations from his tummy of hunger, satiety and gas

Once you appreciate the sensory implications of feeding and know the difference between calming and distressing stimuli, feeding time can become a soothing sensory experience for you both. Follow these guidelines:

- Whether you breast- or bottle-feed, keep your baby's sensory environment the same. This means also holding him close when you bottle-feed, so that he experiences your touch. Unwrap your baby and allow his hands to be free to explore your chest, neck or face.
- Just as you move your baby from one breast to the other whilst breast-feeding, alternate the side he feeds on when you bottle-feed. This will ensure that your baby receives sensory input equally on both sides of his body.
- Keep your voice even, so that he hears it as soothing or crooning. Try to avoid anxiety at feeding time as it can cause your voice to be high-pitched.

- Don't wear perfume for the first months of your baby's life when he is in very close proximity to you at a time when smell is important, namely while he is eating. Your own body smell is the most neutral and best for your baby.

- Note how your baby reacts to the taste of your milk. Some babies react negatively to certain strong flavours like garlic or spices that may taint the taste of breast milk. Not all formula milk tastes the same; if your baby fusses at feed time, he may not like the taste. Consider this when discussing a change of formula with your clinic adviser.

- Be cautious with any extra sensory input you give your baby while he's feeding. He may be able to focus on only the intricate co-ordination of sucking, swallowing and breathing. If you choose to talk to him, do so quietly and calmly. Don't poke and prod him. Rather keep your touch a still, deep hug. Picture the scenario of the baby who is feeding well, when Mom starts to talk to him. He loses focus and his sucking becomes uncoordinated, so he fusses at the breast a bit. Mom reads this as a wind and takes him off the breast to wind him. He is still hungry, so he cries. She reads this as a big wind, bounces him, changes position and pats harder. The result: he is still hungry, but too over-stimulated to feed well, the feed is aborted and he's hungry for his next feed sooner than he should be.

- Wind is internal sensory input, and the presence of gas may push your baby into sensory overload. When he has a wind, he may automatically unlatch off the breast, or spit the teat of the bottle out. Wait a few minutes for a wind to break and then continue the feed. Don't worry if he doesn't produce a very audible wind. Some babies do not break wind very loudly, whereas others' efforts would make their dads proud! Recommence the second half of the feed after a few minutes, regardless of whether he produces a wind or not.

- Learn to read your baby's signals while he is feeding. If he makes eye-contact, reciprocate, but as soon as he looks away, you follow suit. This will allow him 'sensory space' to focus on the task at hand. When he is indeed hungry and is well-rested, he will most likely find the sensory stimuli during feeding calming and soothing and he will feed well.

DEMAND FEEDING

Demand feeding is important in the early weeks to establish an adequate breast milk supply. But unrestrained demand feeding beyond this **does not allow your baby to learn to self-soothe**. In this case, when your baby fusses, you automatically assume that he is hungry and offer him a feed. If he is fussing owing to tiredness or sensory overload, he will suck as a method to self-calm. In this instance his need is in fact for non-nutritive sucking (unless it's time for a feed). But if he is offered a feed every time he fusses, it will set a pattern where he expects his sensory needs to always be met with the offer of a feed. If you rather regulate your baby's environment and offer him other calming methods, he learns that feeding is not the only way of self-calming.

CHAPTER 6

Establish good sleep habits

Diana's mom anticipated waking once a night to feed her in the first few weeks, but she hoped to be having a full night's sleep once Diana was two months old. It's not surprising that six weeks into motherhood she feels disappointed and despondent about still having to get up two to three times at night. It may have been easier for her if she had been more realistic about her baby's needs.

Sleep is vital for our physical and emotional well-being. Sleep deprivation has been used for many centuries as a most effective means of torture, yet countless parents of young children endure this on a daily basis. But helping your baby establish good sleep habits will ensure that the period of sleep deprivation lasts no longer than absolutely necessary. And knowing what to expect during those first few weeks will help you cope better with a lack of sleep.

- Expect to suffer from some sleep deprivation for the first three months at least. So try to sleep when your baby sleeps – even during the day.
- A content, happy and healthy newborn baby may wake frequently for feeding, so expect to wake two- to three-hourly during the night for the first few weeks. Gradually the stretches between night feeds lengthen, so that by three to four months of age, your baby should be able to last for up to eight hours without a feed.

SLEEP CYCLES

It is important to understand the pathways of sleep, as this will give you a clearer understanding of your baby's behaviour.

Sleep is divided into light or REM (rapid eye movement) sleep and deep or non-REM sleep. Deep sleep is when we sleep soundly, whereas during light sleep a knock at the door may easily wake us. This sleep cycle, ranging from the drowsy through light sleep into deep sleep and then back into light sleep, lasts from about 45 to 90 minutes in total. A baby's cycle lasts approximately 45 minutes, increasing to about 90 minutes in adulthood. During a full night's sleep we pass through the sleep cycle many times, drifting back into deep sleep from light sleep, thereby linking sleep cycles.

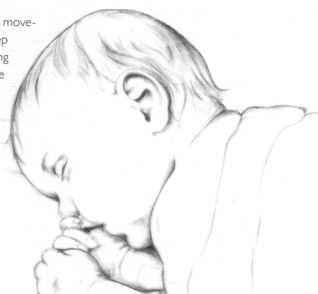

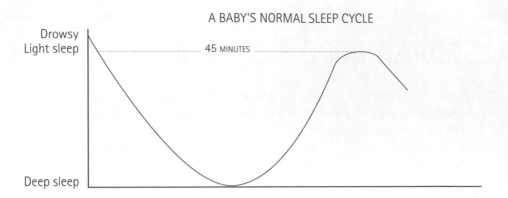

A BABY'S NORMAL SLEEP CYCLE

Drowsy
Light sleep .... 45 MINUTES ....

Deep sleep

Age-appropriate times for sleep

As tempting as it is to throw yourself and your baby headlong into a rigid routine, this is not sensible in the early days. Having said that, from about six weeks most babies can start to develop a pattern to their day sleeps. A flexible routine for day sleeps can be easily established by watching how long your baby has been awake. The time from waking until your baby needs her next sleep is limited simply by her age, for example a newborn can only cope with short periods (45 minutes) of awake time stimulation and interaction. As your baby gets older, she will be able to stay awake for longer and longer periods.

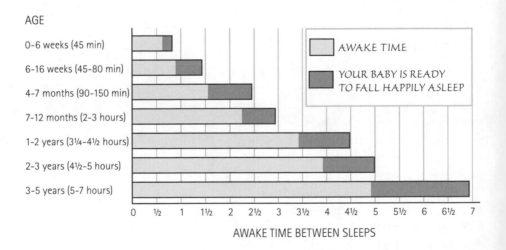

AGE

| 0-6 weeks (45 min) |
| 6-16 weeks (45-80 min) |
| 4-7 months (90-150 min) |
| 7-12 months (2-3 hours) |
| 1-2 years (3¼-4½ hours) |
| 2-3 years (4½-5 hours) |
| 3-5 years (5-7 hours) |

AWAKE TIME

YOUR BABY IS READY
TO FALL HAPPILY ASLEEP

0   ½   1   1½   2   2½   3   3½   4   4½   5   5½   6   6½   7

AWAKE TIME BETWEEN SLEEPS

Abnormal sleep habits

Some babies do not establish regular sleep cycles. They catnap and never sleep for longer than 60 minutes without waking. When such a baby moves into Light Sleep, she is unable to move back into Deep Sleep and so becomes fully awake. She never links one sleep cycle to the next. This results in poor sleep habits and a baby who is irritable and over-tired when awake.

We know that while they are awake babies take in a great deal of stimulation. They need sleep to process all the information received. If a baby does not get sufficient sleep to reset her sensory system, she tends to wake up grumpy and fractious, with few or no 'approach – play with me' signals. Waking before she is fully rested means that she is more likely to become over-stimulated during the following awake period. Not all babies need to sleep for long, so if your baby is a catnapper but is happy and content, don't worry about it.

Since the sleep cycle lasts about 45 minutes it is imperative that you allow your baby to sleep for at least this long or even more during some day sleeps. At some times during the day an older baby may need just a catnap, a shorter sleep, in order to feel rested. This is usually the early morning, or late afternoon nap. But it is important that she has a longer stretch of sleep at least once during the day and, of course, at night.

If your baby is getting enough sleep, and is developing the ability to regulate her sleep states, she will move smoothly from a state of Deep Sleep, through Light Sleep to a Calm-Alert state several times a day.

SET THE STAGE FOR SLEEP

The secret to ensuring that your baby develops good sleep habits is to get off on the right foot from the very beginning by setting the stage for sleep.

Limit awake time

Follow your baby's age-appropriate awake time and, as she approaches the end of that time, put her to sleep. Her signals will also indicate when she is ready for sleep and should be observed so that you get to know when she is tired before she becomes fractious and over-stimulated (see page 33). Day sleeps are important. You will find guidelines for flexible daytime routines, according to six age-bands, in the Chapters 11-16.

It is important that you limit your baby's **awake time** and that she sleeps as much as she needs to and when she needs to. If your baby does not get enough sleep, she will become over-tired, fuss more, and be less likely to fall asleep easily at her sleep times. Always follow the guidelines for awake time (see table).

Establish a sleep zone

In the very early days, it does not matter where your baby sleeps. Provided that her physical and sensory needs are being adequately met, she will most likely spend most of the time sleeping and eating. However, from around the age of three months, it is important that you establish a consistent sleep zone that she will learn to recognize as such.

Where you choose this sleep zone to be is really up to you, but it is important that it is calming and that you are consistent about putting your baby to sleep in this area.

> SENSE-ABLE SECRET
> To help your baby develop healthy sleep habits, day sleeps should also be taken in her own bed whenever possible.

Regulate your baby's sensory environment

If your baby is in a calm environment, she will be calmer through the day and therefore more ready for sleep in the evening. Over-stimulation during the day is a big contributor to night wakings. Ensure that your baby is not being over-stimulated and that she has some space to be calm and alert during the day.

Regulating your baby's environment also means ensuring that her room supports sleep. Ideas for a calming sleep environment include:

• white noise
• a stuffed toy or piece of clothing that smells of parent
• lullabies
• a dark room at night and closed curtains for daytime naps.

Bedtime routine

Babies thrive on routine, so having the identical bedtime routine every night will soon become a sleep signal for her. Try to keep this time of the day quiet and calm, so if Dad is home, there should be no excitement or horseplay but rather calming, nurturing interactions.

Specific activities starting an hour before bedtime will trigger your baby to begin to prepare for sleep.

• A calming, warm bath. Add a drop of lavender or camomile oil.
• Wrap her tightly in a warm towel to be dried.
• Massage her (see page 91) in her dimly lit sleep space.
• Maintain a calm atmosphere at all times. Play some calming lullaby music.
• Don't take her out of the bedroom again; instead play quietly on the floor with her or read to her.
• When you give her her last feed, turn the lights off and complete the feed in the dark.

Put your baby to bed awake, but drowsy

This is an important principle. From about three months on, babies develop sleep associations – they learn to associate falling asleep with certain sensory input. If you rock your baby to sleep at night, she will learn that that is the stimulus she needs to fall asleep. This situation may suit you when you are putting her to sleep, but the downside is that when she wakes during the night she will need that same association to fall back asleep again. Rocking her to sleep may not suit you quite as well at 2 am.

Putting your baby to bed awake, but drowsy, prevents excessive night wakings when she is older. Give her a security object (such as a soft toy or small blanket) and say good night before going out of the room. A security object is a good sleep association, as it will help your baby fall back asleep independently when she wakes during the night.

All babies wake frequently during the night, even those who sleep through. The fact is that most babies wake every 45 to 90 minutes throughout the night. Good sleepers wake up into a very light sleep or drowsy state, but do not rouse, or wake fully. They may just stir and turn over or call out once and go back to sleep. Should they wake up fully, they may sit up and then use finger-sucking, or holding and snuggling down with a security object or a similar method to go back to sleep independently.

Poor sleepers wake up in the same way, but are unable to shift back to sleep without an external stimulus, such as sucking on the breast, bottle or dummy, or being rocked.

SLEEP SOLUTIONS

If night wakings continue beyond the age when your baby needs a night feed (until about six months), you will need to tackle the problem.

The solution begins with satisfying any basic needs or addressing medical problems that may prevent your baby from developing good sleep habits. Often this is all that's needed to improve your baby's sleep habits. (See Process of elimination on page 56.) Basic needs include hunger, thirst and wet or dirty nappies, all of which need to be ruled out.

A sick baby will battle to sleep well because of discomfort, pain or irritability. A blocked nose and earache are among the common causes of night wakings.

Separation anxiety

Some babies develop sleep problems associated with anxiety about being apart from their mothers. This usually only develops at around eight months of age. Should your baby become unduly anxious whenever you are out of sight, you need to help her learn that you are still there for her even when she can't see you and that you do return to her after separations. During her awake time during the day, play the kind of games that normalize separation and teach her that you still exist, even if she can't see you. These games include:
- Peek-a-boo.
- Saying 'bye-bye', going out of the room and then returning.
- Hide-and-seek.
- Hiding objects and helping her find them.

Sleep coaching

When sleep deprivation caused by night wakings affects your health and well-being to the extent that your role as care-giver becomes compromised or is making your baby very irritable during the day, sleep coaching may well be the best option. There may be times when your baby will cry and protest the breaking of old habits while you are teaching her to sleep through the night. But following these simple guidelines will minimize the stress for both you and your baby.

UNDER SIX MONTHS

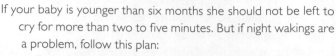

If your baby is younger than six months she should not be left to cry for more than two to five minutes. But if night wakings are a problem, follow this plan:

- Ensure that the stage is set for sleep.
  - Check whether she has any basic needs or illness to be taken care of.
  - Having done this, give her a chance to settle independently by letting her fuss for up to five minutes. Note that this is not full-blown crying, but the tired niggling just before she falls asleep.
    - If she does not settle, go to her and give her her hands or dummy to suck, snuggle her up to a favourite blanket or security object or turn her onto her side. You may have to gently stroke or pat her, saying "ssh-ssh-ssh" for a while until she is calm.
      - If she moves into a real crying state, meet her emotional needs immediately by picking her up, holding her close to you, and gently rocking her until she is calm. Put her back in her cot when she is calm and drowsy, but not yet asleep.
      - If she has been asleep and wakes crying, try to settle her by saying "ssh-ssh-ssh" and gently stroking or patting her until she is calm. Encourage her to suck on her hands or a dummy, tuck in her security object and shift her position. If she does not settle after a minute or two, pick her up, hold her close to you and gently rock her until she is calm.
- Continue in this manner until she is asleep. This may take a bit of time, so be prepared to "work with her" until you get it right, both at bedtime and during the night when she wakes.

OVER SIX MONTHS

If your baby has learnt to fall asleep only while feeding or being rocked or held, or simply having you close by, she may cry and cry until you return to these old habits. In this case you may need to let her cry a little, while she learns new strategies to self-soothe and put herself to sleep.

- First set the stage for good sleep habits. This may take a day or two to set up and must be done before starting sleep coaching.
- Hunger may be an issue in night waking and, indeed, in restless days. Breast-fed babies need more frequent feeding than bottle-fed ones, and those that are already on solids are not as hungry as those that have not yet started eating solid food. Each case is different, but hunger must be excluded before any form of sleep coaching can be implemented. It is only possible to exclude hun-

ger entirely once your baby is having solid food and is on a diet that includes protein. This should only happen when she is six to seven months old.

- Before letting your baby cry, you must take her to your family doctor or a paediatrician for a full check-up, to rule out any medical reason for night waking, such as ear and throat infections, which are common causes.
- Try to assist your baby to self-calm by not automatically picking her up to settle her unless it's feed time. In this case the feed must involve minimal interaction and no light, unless she is sick – then all rules go out the window (as does sleep).
- Finally, before you begin sleep coaching, there must be agreement between you and your partner on commitment to a sleep-coaching method. If there is any disagreement, you are better off waiting until you agree. Otherwise you will not have the support you need and will be less likely to be consistent with the programme. Inconsistency is a big problem, as it gives your baby very mixed messages. It will do more harm than good if sometimes she's left to cry and other times she's 'put' to sleep.

FALLING ASLEEP INDEPENDENTLY

Your goal is to teach your baby to fall asleep without relying on external associations or comforts that require your intervention. She needs to learn self-soothing techniques such as stroking her hair or face, or holding a security object like a small teddy or a soft, cotton blanket.

- Start by limiting the amount of time you spend holding, rocking or singing to your baby before bedtime. Ensure she is drowsy, but not fully asleep, when you put her in her cot.
- Put your baby down happily awake (drowsy) and leave the room.
- If she begins to fuss or cry, allow her two to five minutes to self-soothe and fall asleep on her own.
- If she doesn't settle, go to her, speak to her in a quiet and soothing manner, and gently stroke or pat her back.
- If she doesn't settle within the next few minutes, the next step of sleep coaching may be necessary. Since this step will involve some crying, some moms choose to stay with their baby while others choose to have short periods of 'time out', away from their baby.
- **If you decide to stay with your baby**, sit with her and put a hand on her. Don't move your hand and don't talk, except to say "ssh-ssh-ssh" quietly and repetitively. She may cry for up to 20 minutes (or even longer the first time). You should sit with her if you can. It is important that you have the confidence to sit alongside your crying baby without resorting to the habit that you are trying to break. You may need to occasionally pick her up to comfort and calm her before placing her back into her cot in a drowsy state to continue with the sleep coaching.
  - Do this each time she wakes during the first night.
  - The next night, or when you are ready to move to the next stage, sit next

to her and don't touch her. Still soothe her with your presence and voice.

○ The following nights, or when you are ready to move to this stage, move further from the cot so that she can feel your presence and hear your voice but is learning to go to sleep on her own. Within as few as four nights you should be able to leave the room. She may have a 'protest night', approximately a week down the line, when she will again cry for longer and need your presence in the room once more.

• **If you would rather be out of the room**, say good night and leave the room, knowing that you will return to comfort your baby when she needs you. This method differs from the first method in that you actually leave the room for short periods of time from the outset. If you feel that you could possibly harm your baby physically (out of sheer exhaustion and frustration), this method allows you to take a deep breath and step away from the situation for short periods of time to re-focus. If your baby cries, leave her for one minute. After one minute, go in, pick her up to comfort her and calm her. When she is calm, lay her back down again, saying a few soothing words, then leave the room (even if she begins to cry once more). This time, wait for two minutes before going back in. If necessary, repeat the procedure, each time adding two more minutes of crying time before going back in to soothe or settle her.

○ Once again, the results will be similar. Within a few nights she will not need your presence to fall asleep. Again, be prepared for a 'protest night' a week down the line. Handle it in the same calm manner.

○ Some babies gag and may even vomit whilst they are crying. Don't be alarmed if this happens (you know your baby is not sick), so do not respond anxiously. When you return to comfort your baby, do not make a big issue of cleaning up — simply place a clean towel under her.

The secrets of success

Rest assured that, as long as her basic needs are consistently and timeously met, gentle and sensitive sleep coaching to teach her to put herself to sleep will have no long-term emotional consequences.

• Expect her to have more periods of unsettledness than actual sleep for the first few sessions, perhaps even for a night or two.
• Be prepared for her nights to get worse before they improve, but persevere.
• Be loving and giving, but remain firm and consistent.
• Spend some extra time during the day playing and cuddling with her. It will do you both the world of good.

The ingredients of the magic recipe for good sleep habits are setting the stage, checking basic needs and, if necessary, sleep coaching.

CHAPTER 7

Crying

Eric was a few weeks old when he changed from being a model baby (feeding three-hourly and sleeping between feeds with only two night wakings) to the fussy baby his mother has come to know. Now when Eric cries, her stomach knots up and a fine layer of perspiration breaks out on her skin. At two in the morning, when he wakes for the sixth time and she doesn't know how long it will take to settle him again, she can feel her agitated heartbeat drumming in her head and the adrenalin pumping through her veins. This is the physical experience of a mother when her baby cries.

Eric's mom put her career on hold and taking care of Eric is her primary role right now – a role in which she feels pressurized to excel. Once a successful journalist in control of her world, she now feels controlled by the two tiny lungs that bellow forth seemingly around the clock. Eric cries so much that everyone, including his mom, thinks she is somehow not meeting his needs. His granny is quick to ask if he's hungry and Dad keeps wondering aloud if Eric is ill. His mom is starting to think that she is just a bad mother.

It's not surprising that she is showing signs of depression. For some weeks she hasn't slept for longer than two hours at a stretch, and she is not getting the gratification of a happy, smiling baby. But she is far from alone. In the modern world where women are used to the positive feedback associated with a successful career, a fussy baby often elicits feelings of frustration and inadequacy in the new mother.

Crying evokes powerful emotions. It's probably the first sound you heard from your little one and, like many parents, you found that it brought tears of joy to your eyes. But a few weeks down the line the sound of crying may evoke feelings far from joy.

NORMAL CRYING

All babies cry. Crying is a very clear form of communication and is essential for survival. Crying is relatively minimal in most babies for the first two weeks, but then increases until it peaks at about six weeks. Thereafter it decreases until at three months it drops off markedly. Babies and toddlers continue to use this form of communication when distressed until well into childhood.

Research shows that both how much babies cry and a mother's perception of how much crying is normal, are extremely variable. Some babies cry for only an hour altogether in a day, while others cry for up to six hours on end. For many mothers even an hour's crying feels excessive.

How a mother copes with crying and how much crying it takes to push her to desperation also vary. The constant factor when it comes to crying is that every mother wants to settle her baby as quickly as possible.

Crying in the early days

When your baby is crying inconsolably every well-meaning aunt and every shop-keeper has a reason and a solution. You can just dismiss comments such as *She's an anxious mother, You drank too much coffee during your pregnancy, Boys cry more than girls* and *He's just spoilt.* The real reasons for crying may be one or more of the following:

- hunger
- tiredness
- over-stimulation
- discomfort caused by a dirty nappy; digestive disturbances such as cramps, bloating, reflux, indigestion, constipation, diarrhoea or over-feeding; medical conditions (which include congenital abnormalities and the like); allergies, for example, eczema; being too hot or too cold
- feeling lonely – the need to be touched, soothed and spoken to.

Of these reasons hunger, tiredness and over-stimulation are the most common in young babies. But how do you determine the reason for your baby's crying? By going through a process of elimination you can identify what is bothering your child at that time. Of course as your baby gets older, you will also come to understand and interpret his cries and that, too, will help you identify the reason for his discomfort.

PROCESS OF ELIMINATION

This is only a guideline to help you find the cause of your crying baby's distress. Each issue is discussed briefly. If the crying persists or you are concerned, you should seek further medical information and assistance.

Environmental discomfort

The first step is to eliminate any discomfort caused by a dirty nappy. Always check your baby's nappy to be sure that he is dry and comfortable. Your baby may also be under- or over-dressed, there may be a cold wind on his face or ears, or direct sunlight may be dazzling him and make him too hot.

Hunger

Parents are often told that the main cause for crying in a small baby is hunger. "Always offer a feed first" is the most frequently given advice, "and only thereaf-ter move on to investigate other reasons". But how do you really know whether your baby is hungry, or crying for another reason? In the first six weeks of life, your baby needs to feed frequently (two- to three-hourly). His tummy is still small and he cannot manage large quantities of milk. From the age of six weeks to four months, he will take in larger quantities of milk and will not need to feed as frequently. From about four months you can add solids to his diet and from six months milk feeds become less frequent (three times a day), as solids take precedence. Your baby's crying could be caused by hunger if:

- It is more than two to three hours since the end of his last feed. This period will increase as he grows.
- You are breast-feeding and your breasts did not feel full at the start of his last feed or he's fussy between feeds, only settling when he has more frequent milk feeds.
- He slept longer than usual between feeds in the preceding 12-24 hours and now needs to 'catch up' on food.
- He is consistently finishing his bottle and still appears to be looking for more.
- He is having a growth spurt, which usually occurs at four, eight and 12 weeks, then again at four, six and nine months.
- He is above average weight for his age, resulting in greater energy needs.
- He has fewer than five to six wet nappies a day.
- He is not gaining weight adequately.

Digestive disturbances

Digestive disturbances are relatively uncommon in breast-fed babies.

FORMULA MILK

If your baby is bottle-fed, the formula you have chosen may not be suitable for him and may be causing him to be unsettled. If your baby's formula is suitable, he will be happy and content between feeds, he will have at least five to six wet nappies a day and he will be gaining weight adequately. If his formula is not suitable he will be restless and unsettled all the time, usually worse in the first hour after his feed. In addition, he may

- vomit after a feed
- have diarrhoea or constipation
- have eczema on his face and body
- fail to thrive (although this does not always occur)
- produce excessive mucus and become congested.

SENSITIVE STOMACH

Many babies have an immature digestive system when they are born (especially premature babies) and, depending on whether they are breast- or bottle-fed, they may be sensitive to either something that Mom might have eaten, or certain ingredients of the formula milk. The main culprit is lactose – the sugar found in both breast milk and any cow's milk modified formula. Babies need the enzyme lactase to digest lactose. In some infants there may not be enough lactase present at birth to digest the lactose, resulting in digestive discomfort, explosive stools and general unsettledness. As the digestive system matures, the production of lactase increases. Most babies grow out of this sensitivity within a few months. If you are breast-feeding, simply eliminating any dairy products from your diet may address the problem. If you are bottle-feeding, switch to a lactose-free formula.

True lactose intolerance is a very rare condition and babies suffering from it are usually unwell, fail to thrive and have constant diarrhoea. Specialist intervention is necessary.

CONSTIPATION

True constipation is unusual in babies. If your baby is simply not producing a stool daily, this is not a sign of constipation. Babies' bowel habits can be very irregular, especially in the early days. Depending on what you are feeding your baby, he may stool after each feed or much less frequently, sometimes going days without passing a stool. Most babies strain a bit when they pass a stool, and if the stool is soft and appears without too much fussing and crying, your baby is not constipated. But if your baby is fussy and uncomfortable, strains to pass a stool, and his stools are hard, small pellets, he may be constipated, which may well be a cause of crying and fussing. Constipation may result from a mild sensitivity to a particular formula, or not enough liquid intake. Some medical conditions also cause constipation. For this reason chronic constipation needs further investigation. Hard stools may also cause a slight tear in the anus which can cause great discomfort. Ask your clinic sister for advice.

REFLUX

In babies suffering from this disorder, the valve between the stomach and the oesophagus (the food pipe to the stomach) is often underdeveloped. It will strengthen with age, but meanwhile the milk is constantly being regurgitated from the stomach into the oesophagus. This in itself does not bother most babies, which is why you may find your baby is a 'happy puker'. But if the acidic milk curds irritate the oesophagus it may cause extreme discomfort and, in some cases, excessive possetting (regurgitating curdled milk) or even projectile vomiting. Occasionally a baby with reflux shows no visible evidence of possetting. These babies cry from the discomfort of the regurgitated stomach acid burning the oesophagus.

Keeping your baby upright, limiting handling after a feed, a change of formula and medication can all help, but essentially it is something that your baby will outgrow with time. There is nothing to worry about, provided he is thriving and gaining weight. Surgery is sometimes required, but fortunately this is rare.

Allergies

There is no doubt that allergies are more prevalent among children of our present generation. If you suspect that your baby's crying may be caused by an allergy, you need to establish whether your baby is just mildly sensitive to a substance, or truly allergic. True allergies cause an immune-system reaction. When the body mistakenly regards a particular substance (allergen) as a foreign invader the immune system responds by producing specific antibodies to this substance. While nothing may happen the first time the allergen is eaten, breathed in or absorbed through the skin, the next time exposure occurs the immune system releases massive amounts of antibodies to protect the body. These antibodies can trigger a cascade of allergic symptoms that can affect the digestive and respiratory systems, and may also affect the skin. These symptoms include diarrhoea, constipation, vomiting, reflux, eczema, a blocked nose and a wheezing chest.

Food intolerance is easily confused with food allergy. Food intolerance is a reaction of the body to certain foods (such as some preservatives or additives). A significant proportion of feeding problems in babies is related to lactose intolerance and cow's milk or soya-bean protein intolerance. Most babies outgrow food intolerances and allergies by the time they reach the toddler stage.

Babies with severe allergic eczema will certainly cry with pain, itching and discomfort, as will a child who has developed a secondary bacterial infection in his upper respiratory tract due to excessive mucous production stemming from an allergic reaction to pollen or certain foodstuffs. If there is a history of allergies in your family it is advisable to have your baby examined by a specialist. Seek medical advice if your baby has any of the above symptoms.

Congenital abnormalities

Congenital abnormalities are present from birth and some may contribute to excessive crying in the first year of life. For example, a cleft palate and a harelip cause major feeding problems from birth. Apart from the discomfort, your baby may be crying from hunger resulting from ineffective feeding. When reconstructive surgery takes place, there will be crying from pain experienced post-operatively.

Some congenital abnormalities have neurological implications, for example Hirschsprung's disease, a neurological disorder of the rectum, which results in constipation. Some rare digestive metabolic disorders can also cause digestive discomfort resulting in excessive crying.

Candida infection

Thrush, caused by the fungus *Candida albicans*, may occur not only in your baby's mouth or on the genital or anal areas, but also in the digestive tract. Oral thrush can cause pain in your baby's mouth and throat when he sucks, while thrush on the genital and anal areas causes a red, itchy and inflamed skin rash. In both cases your baby may cry and be fretful. Anti-fungal treatment may be necessary for you and your baby, as well as replacing the friendly bacteria by means of a pro-biotic to restore intestinal balance. Seek guidance from your clinic adviser.

If your baby has a noisy, rumbling and bloated tummy and you suspect that systemic thrush may be the culprit, consult your medical practitioner.

Illness

One of the first indications that your baby is unwell will be his reluctance to feed. Aversion to the odd feed (once every now and then, maybe once a week) is quite normal – provided he is thriving and gaining weight. But consistent fussing at feed time is cause for concern.

If your baby has a viral or bacterial infection, he will be irritable. He may have obvious symptoms such as a fever, rash, chesty cough, diarrhoea or vomiting. If he has an ear infection, he may fuss or scream when moved out of the upright position. This is because raised fluid or pus levels in his ear canal may cause pressure and pain when he lies flat. Sucking may also trigger this pain, so he may appear hungry, but cry once he starts to feed. All these symptoms need to be investigated further.

A limp, quieter than normal baby is always cause for concern. Investigate immediately – and seek help.

Spinal pain

We all know the pain and discomfort of neck and backache. But what we don't realise is that babies can suffer from it too. Occasionally this is the simple reason why you have an unsettled baby.

Mal-alignment of the spine, causing pain and discomfort, may have resulted from a very prolonged labour or an injury your baby suffered at birth. If your baby spends too long sitting in baby seats and not enough time stretched out flat, muscle tightness and joint inflammation can occur, causing spinal discomfort. Muscle tightness and joint inflammation in turn can cause irritability of the nervous system. This may lead to impaired digestive function and a baby who suffers from gas and cramps. Consider having your baby evaluated by a registered chiropractor who specializes in the treatment of babies if you suspect that his crying is caused by spinal pain.

Trauma

Any physical trauma experienced by your baby will obviously result in pain and crying. Trauma may be caused by accidents (motor vehicle, in the home, unusual natural events), birth injury or child abuse. Babies are incredibly intuitive and will certainly pick up and react to any emotional trauma experienced by you.

Separation anxiety

Some babies develop sleep problems associated with anxiety about being apart from their mothers. This has been discussed at length on page 51.

CAUTION

This information is not meant to take the place of medical information available from your doctor. If in any doubt, seek further medical advice immediately.

Fussing and colic

The twins were Sue's third pregnancy and, after getting over the shock of carrying not just a third but a fourth baby, she felt that she would cope well, as she was an old hand at the mothering game. So it was with great misgivings that she realized, when the boys were a month old, that she did not have all the answers. Steven, the elder twin, was a dream, sleeping when he should and generally fitting into a routine with ease. Michael, on the other hand, was the challenge that Sue had never anticipated.

He did not take to the breast and within a week was being bottle-fed. He couldn't differentiate between day and night for a long time and kept Sue up most nights. She was in despair and totally exhausted, as Michael did not ever sleep for longer than forty minutes at a stretch and when he woke, he did so screaming as though in pain. She suddenly realized what colic was all about.

Despite being twins, they were so different. Steven was a plump and contented-looking baby, but Michael cried so much that no one really found him very endearing. Like most people, Sue found herself wondering how two babies, cared for by the same mother, could be poles apart in behaviour.

Each of us has a different capacity for stimulation that determines how we react to sensory information. Likewise at different times of day or when we are stressed we may respond differently to stimulation. If we have a low capacity to cope with sensory input, a small and seemingly insignificant stimulus may be overwhelming and affect our behaviour. This is never more apparent in our lives than during babyhood. A baby's capacity to take in, filter and organize the sensory input he is exposed to, determines his behaviour and how he will respond to the world.

VARYING THRESHOLDS

Some babies respond appropriately to sensory information, filter sensory information well and are good at communicating, using their unique baby signals. These babies adapt with ease and can self-calm, leaving them emotionally available to bond and interact with the world.

Other babies seem totally under-responsive, hardly noticing any sensory changes in the environment. Because these babies filter sensory information to a great extent, they are often considered 'very easy' or 'good' babies.

Then there are babies who react to **any** sensory input or changes in the environment by becoming increasingly disorganized and fussing terribly. These sensitive babies have great difficulty regulating their state and signalling when they have had enough. If your baby fusses constantly and appears to suffer from colic more severely than other babies, he may belong to this group.

Irritability
Gaze-aversion or gaze-locking
Finger-splaying/saluting
Squirming, appearing to 'sit on air'
Back- and neck-arching, appearing
  to 'push away'
Frantic, disorganized, jerky
  movements
Frowning
Tongue-thrusting

Grimacing, frowning and grunting
Yawning, sneezing or hiccups
Colour changes – paleness,
  mottling, flushing, blueness
  around the mouth
Faster heart rate and panting
Gagging, spitting-up
Whimpering and fussing
Crying

COLIC

Colic is a term that is bandied about and used as a broad umbrella term for all kinds of distressed behaviour in the first year. Traditionally *colic* referred to a period of extended crying. As the term caught on, it began to be synonymous with digestive disturbances and even just mild windy tummies. The general dictionary definition of colic is 'severe spasmodic abdominal pain'. Understood as such, it is the cause most commonly attributed to periods of extended crying in the first year.

Demystifying colic

Theories abound on the reasons for colic, ranging from reflux, lactose intolerance and excessive gas to spinal misalignment and an overly anxious mother. The reality is that there is no conclusive evidence that any of these are the cause of colic. In fact, research on the 'cures' based on these explanations, such as colic or reflux medication, counselling and over-the-counter drops for alleviating winds have all been shown to be as effective (or ineffective) as sugar pills, in other words nothing really works. Furthermore, none of these ideas would explain why colic is classically experienced in the evening. Take for instance abdominal gas. We now know that nearly all babies have gas or winds after feeds and that this 'gas' is no worse after an evening feed than a morning feed. Yet only some babies respond to this irritation by displaying 'colicky' behaviour. This is because every baby has his own particular threshold level at which sensory input becomes over-stimulating and causes disorganization or sensory overload.

Sensory overload can lead to colic

Colic can occur at any time during the day, but is most common at the end of the day. Your baby receives sensory input throughout the day. At certain times, usually at the end of the day, between 5 pm and 9 pm, but also after a particularly stimulating event, your baby reaches his threshold. When his threshold is low and he is over-stimulated, his body releases stress hormones. This results in a 'flight or fight' response which alerts and arouses your baby, contributing to his fussy state at this time. At this point a small stimulus, such as bath time, Dad coming home or just a full tummy, may be enough to push him over the edge, which is when a colic episode may occur. The offending stimulation at this time of day is frequently internal sensory input.

At this time a little regurgitation of milk or the small gas bubbles in your baby's stomach, with which he coped and could ignore at 10 am, are the final straw at 5 pm and push him over the edge into a scream. He will frequently pull up his legs as if in digestive pain, which is why many people say gas causes colic. But, in fact, it is the internal sensory input (of the gas) that contributes to over-stimulation. On other days it may not be the gas – it may be a loud restaurant or a scratchy label in your baby's vest that is the catalyst for a colic episode.

Inappropriate response can aggravate colic

What happens next determines how long the colic will last. How you handle the fussing determines whether your baby fusses for 15 minutes or settles in for a three-hour stretch.

It is understandable that you may become anxious, anticipating a crying spell similar to one you had to cope with the night before. You may start to wind your baby vigorously. The bouncing and patting only serve to further stimulate him. Then you turn on the light or take him into the TV room so that you can be sociable while trying to calm your baby, further exacerbating the problem. You try singing, talking, lying down, offering another feed, changing the nappy, holding your baby in various positions, until finally your exhausted baby plunges into

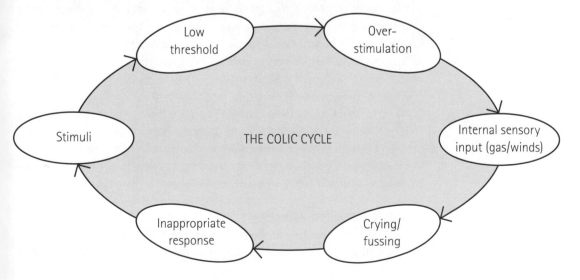

THE COLIC CYCLE

Low threshold → Over-stimulation → Internal sensory input (gas/winds) → Crying/fussing → Inappropriate response → Stimuli → Low threshold

sleep. Although each strategy is valid if the timing is appropriate, to a baby with an already over-stimulated system this barrage of well-meant attempts to calm him is more likely to contribute to further over-stimulation. But if you stay calm and use the principles of sensory calming, your baby is much more likely to fall asleep without too much crying.

HOW TO CALM YOUR FUSSING BABY

First check through the process of elimination and take care of basic needs or any medical problems. If sufficient time has passed since the last feed and hunger is the cause for crying, **feed** your baby. During or shortly after feed time, gas can build up, making your baby uncomfortable. **Burp** him for a short time but do not become over-concerned about winds that are not easily brought up. If you try too hard to wind your baby, you are likely to push him into sensory overload and make him more uncomfortable. Burp him for no more than five minutes; if no burp emerges, do not be concerned – it will come out the other end.

Check his nappy. If your baby has a very wet or dirty nappy the tactile discomfort may be enough to make him uncomfortable. So change those dirty nappies as soon as you become aware of them.

Implement a **flexible routine** if you are not yet following any daytime routine. This will make your baby's cries more predictable. Understanding his needs from the outset is often the secret to calming a fussy baby. Most fussy babies are over-tired and over-stimulated.

Day sleeps are crucial for keeping a baby calm most of his waking hours. Use the guidelines for awake time on page 48 and follow the flexible routine appropriate for your baby's age (see Chapters 11-16).

Calming strategies

When calming your baby, the appropriate **timing** of the strategy is as important as the **choice** of calming strategy. Bear in mind your baby's state when going through the process of elimination and implementing the calming strategies. If he is clearly over-tired or over-stimulated, a barrage of input may only lead to further overload. For this reason choose only one strategy and stick to it for a while before trying another. Sometimes all your baby needs is sleep – in that case every bit of stimulation will only make matters worse.

When in doubt, take a deep breath and try one basic needs solution (such as checking the nappy or burping – if appropriate). Then try the calming strategies detailed below to help him calm down for sleep or settle him. Use each one for five minutes before changing to the next strategy, as your baby's system will take a while to adjust and calm down with each change.

REGULATE THE ENVIRONMENT

Establish whether anything in the environment is over-stimulating your baby. It may be a strong perfume or a high-pitched voice or the bright fluorescent lights of a supermarket. By being in tune with your baby's signals, you will know when to remove him from a stimulus and also which stimuli to avoid in future. Moving your baby into a dimly-lit, quiet room may be all that he needs to calm down.

SELF-CALMING

A baby can begin to self-calm from a young age – even a few weeks old. If he is never allowed the opportunity to learn to self-calm, he will never master the art. This will happen if you instantly react to every murmur or squeak your baby makes. That is not to say that babies must be left to cry. It means that you should first watch for your baby to show signs of his ability to self-calm and encourage this skill to develop by allowing him to calm himself if he's on the right track.

Sucking his hands or fists	Certain body positions (he may
Touching his face, hair	prefer lying on his left or right)
or ears	Looking at his hands
Gazing at you or any object	Bringing his hands together or in
that appears to calm him	towards the midline

MASSAGE

Touch is a tool that mothers use intuitively with their babies, from the soft caress of a kiss on his silky head to a deep hug or swaddling in a cotton blanket when your baby is fractious. For a fussy baby touch can be used therapeutically as a daily massage.

There are many different approaches to baby massage – find the one that works best for you and your baby (see page 91).

MOVEMENT AND TOUCH

Babies love the sense of movement. While some types of movement are stimulatory, other movement, such as that which was experienced in utero, is calming. While in the womb, your baby was lulled with a rocking motion and the deep pressure of the womb walls as he moved. For this reason, when you carry your baby, the movement combined with deep pressure is the most calming input and is what your baby experiences when you walk while carrying him in a baby sling or pouch.

When soothing your fractious baby, rock or pace in time to your heartbeat (approximately 70-72 beats per minute). Better still, placing him in a sling or pouch when he fusses or when you need both hands free, is a great way to keep him calm. Research shows that babies who are carried in baby carriers are significantly less fussy.

VISUAL STIMULATION

There are times during the day when your baby needs a change of scenery. These will occur at various intervals throughout the day, becoming more frequent as he gets older. Make sure that it is not time for a sleep or that your baby is not already over-stimulated before offering visual stimulation. Trees and leaves are natures mobiles and are wonderfully calming. Babies also love to look at photographs of faces.

SOOTHING SOUNDS

Up to six weeks of age, babies find intrauterine or womb sounds very soothing. These sounds or white noise like radio static or the sound of a vacuum cleaner can be sufficient to calm a fussy baby. The rhythm of your heartbeat was of great comfort to your baby for the last six months in the womb, so hold him close to your heart. Interestingly, the majority of parents hold their babies on the left shoulder regardless of their hand preference, indicating that intuitively we hold our babies close to our hearts. Softly played classical or baroque music or gentle lullabies can also soothe a fussy baby. Talk or sing softly to your baby, he loves the sound of your voice.

TAKE A WALK

Put your baby in his pram, sling or pouch and go for a walk. The change of scenery and the benefit of a brisk walk outdoors will do both of you a world of good. Don't let caring for your fussy baby force you into staring at four walls day and night – it is important to have a change of scenery to help you relax and focus on other things.

CALMING YOUR CRYING BABY	Listen to the cry – what does it say? Go through the process of elimination. Look at the sensory environment and the time of day. Act according to your baby's needs. Wait five minutes for a response. Try another solution.

Responding to evening colic

Since colic episodes are more prevalent at the end of the day, usually between 5 pm and 9 pm, preventive strategies to deal with them may make your life a lot easier.

BEDTIME IS CRITICAL

The way you manage the last stretch of the day into early evening is key to limiting colic in the early days and the 'horror hour' you have come to dread. Aim for a period of quiet time from late afternoon which may include a soothing bath, massage and the last feed before bedtime. Always remain aware of how much time your baby has spent awake since his last sleep (see awake times, page 48).

Follow these steps at bedtime:

• Swaddle your baby for the last feed and feed him in his sleep space, in the dark with white noise or calming music playing in the background. Avoid any other stimulation in his environment at this time.

- If he falls asleep by the end of the feed, wind him very gently for a brief time – a maximum of five minutes. If a burp does not emerge do not be concerned.
- Lay your baby on his side in his crib. Encourage non-nutritive sucking such as a dummy or his fingers and place your hand on him with still, deep touch. Avoid frenetic patting or stroking.
- If he wriggles and niggles, encourage non-nutritive sucking, keep your hand firmly on his body, and stay with him until he settles.

RESPONDING AS CRYING BEGINS

If your baby is not settling, pick him up gently and try to settle him in your arms. If he still does not settle, offer him a feed. Many babies settle with a cluster feed at this time, but be conscious not to overfeed as overfeeding can cause discomfort. Keep him swaddled for this feed and do it with a minimum of fuss and stimulation. Wind him gently, but don't be concerned if he does not burp.

- When he has finished feeding, place him in his crib as you did before and keep your hand on him with still and deep touch.
- Give him time to settle out of your arms with touch pressure and the sound of white noise, even if he is wriggling and niggling.

COPING WITH PROLONGED CRYING

If your colicky baby remains unsettled after half an hour, or he continues to scream with no periods of niggling and wriggling, take him out of his crib, re-swaddle him, encourage non-nutritive sucking (dummy or fingers) and soothe him with the lulling movement of your body. You can hold him firmly in your arms to do this, but placing him in a sling works brilliantly. A sling works better than just carrying him because your baby is in a soothing sensory 'bland' space where he is not further stimulated or fiddled with. Stay in the quiet and darkened sleep zone with him and resist the temptation to leave the room, no matter how frustrated and tired you are. Keep him close to you and don't worry about spoiling him, he is little. Once he is asleep you can resettle him in his crib.

Give yourself a break

No one will ever understand the pressure on mothers of fussy babies. There are moments in the day when unthinkable thoughts come to mind. Lack of sleep and the burden of nurturing a baby who is never fully satisfied for long are soul-destroying. You may suffer from depression and feelings of desperation, so a break or time-out is vital! Ask your husband or a supportive family member or neighbour to look after your baby for a short period so that you can take a break. Go and have a massage or take a long walk alone. Try to take a little time each day to soak in a bath or to read a magazine article.

Finally, know this – it will pass. Most babies grow out of the fussy colic stage at around twelve weeks. Those that don't are in the minority and may have a regulatory disorder. But even their irritability decreases with time and their symptoms change as they get older.

REGULATORY DISORDERS

A very small percentage of babies have what we call a regulatory disorder. They have difficulty regulating their moods and states, as well as with self-calming. They display persistent fussing and are hard to calm. They cry for more than three hours a day, more than three days of the week and for a period of longer than three months. The crying persists past the normal three-month colic stage and by six months they are still very fussy and have eating and/or sleep problems. These babies are often particularly sensitive – showing irritability to touch and movement and heightened awareness of sounds and visual input. If your baby fits this description, go through the following process before seeking specialist advice:

- Go through the process of elimination and seek medical advice to rule out any illness or injury.
- If there is no reasonable medical explanation, go through the checklist for a sensory problem and/or regulatory disorder.
(*See* Appendix A, page 151.)
- If there are reasonable indicators that it may be a regulatory disorder or sensory hypersensitivity, contact an occupational therapist who special-izes in sensory integration disorders of infancy or speak to your clinic sister or paediatrician. For names of therapists specialized in sensory integration who treat infants go to http://www.instsi.co.za.

CHAPTER 9

Development and stimulation

"Much of early mothering ... is a matter of modulating the baby's state, warding off stimulation as well as providing it, protecting against excessive doses as well as supplying extra stimuli. The interaction of mother and baby is often treated as a purely emotional affair, yet it appears that certain quite specific aspects also have cognitive - intellectual - implications, in that they enable the baby to attain a level of attentiveness at which he can begin to explore his surroundings and perceptually (later on manipulatively) familiarise himself with the environment... When caretakers do not have the time or sensitivity to help a baby reach a state in which he can maximally profit from encounters with his world, even the richest environment will fail to 'get through'. In the end it is the personal attention involved in picking up rather than a great range of impersonal toys that speeds up developmental progress." Rudolph Schaffer, *Mothering*, 1977.

It's easy to lose perspective both on what is normal in the various stages of development, and on the role of stimulation. So let's look at development and stimulation to enable you to be more sensitive to your baby's state so that "she can maximally profit from encounters" with her world.

DEVELOPMENTAL SKILLS

We differ from other species in so many ways. On a spiritual level, most humans seek answers to the great questions of life. On an intellectual level, we have the ability to read and to increase our knowledge base. Research shows that each generation has a higher average IQ than the previous one. On a physical level there are four distinct developmental skills or areas that separate us from all other species

Gross motor development

We are the only species to use the **upright posture** as the primary position from which to interact with the world. For this we need gross motor development, the term used for the large movements of the body. The primary goal of the gross motor system in the first year is to achieve control against gravity, taking the baby from a helpless, curled-up bundle through the stages of rolling, sitting and crawling, to the mobile toddler we see at around a year.

Fine motor development

We have a wonderfully and **uniquely designed hand** that enables us to manipulate objects of all different shapes and sizes with precision. Furthermore, we can co-ordinate our hands and eyes (eye-hand co-ordination) for precise tasks such as writing. For this we need fine motor skills which include the refined movements of the arms and hands.

Language development

We have a vast **spoken language** and a natural sense of language, which allows us to use words in many contexts without learning each specific context. A chimpanzee can learn to label a stick, but a young child can use the word stick as an adjective, verb and noun. We also have the aptitude to learn more languages than just our mother tongue. Language development includes the reading of non-verbal signals, understanding language, making pre-language sounds and from about one year, speaking.

Social and emotional development

We have **complex social structures** that function for the benefit of the group as well as the individual. We also care for our young for a relatively long period of time. This is possibly the most important area of human development as it allows a baby to form meaningful relationships with, and attachment to, significant caregivers. Emotional development also includes the ability to self-calm and regulate her states.

Milestones

Within each of these primary development areas are specific milestones your baby will achieve in her first year of life. Part two of this book provides details of the milestones in each area for each age-band, followed by suggestions for structuring a sensory environment that will enhance your baby's development and help her reach these milestones.

THE WIDE RANGE OF 'NORMAL'

Every responsible baby-care book will tell you that each baby progresses at her own pace. This is important to remember for many reasons.

Time-spans in which milestones are reached are broad

There is something about being a new parent, especially with a first baby, that brings out a slightly competitive streak. Even if you don't initially suffer from this tendency, some proud mom or dad wheeling a pram in the park will bring it out in you by openly stating that their baby is the most advanced, pretty or clever. So you start watching your baby's milestones closely, looking for any sign of brilliance. But you have to bear in mind that milestones are reached in broad time spans. For example, your baby may start sitting anywhere between five and eight months. Likewise, walking occurs between 10 and 18 months.

Babies are individuals and shouldn't be judged on the achievement of milestones, as this is generally not a reliable predictor of either giftedness or handicap.

Premature babies develop according to their adjusted age – the age they would be if born on their due date. It is easy to work out the adjusted or developmental age:

Age – months premature = adjusted/developmental age

So a six-month-old who was born one month prematurely should be as developed as the typical five-month-old. This applies until the child is about two years old.

Development varies according to aptitude

From an early age, your baby's interests and talents may become evident. Just as you may be a brilliant squash player and your partner a gifted musician, so babies have capacities for different skills. You may find your baby is a social little being who smiles early, talks well and has an ability to make friends and read their emotions astutely as a toddler. Another baby may be shy and socially reserved and spend hours exploring fine-motor activities with great interest. These babies are honing the skills for which they have a special interest and aptitude.

Development varies within the individual

Regardless of aptitude, your baby's development may vary at different times. One week your new baby may be starting to hold her head up and the next week she may seem to lose her head control to a great extent. Some time later, seemingly overnight, your apparently gifted ten-month-old may lose all five words she's been happily gabbling. This phenomenon is called 'competition of skills'. As the different skills develop, they compete for the brain's energy and so the focus of the brain's energy shifts. Your baby may be focusing on language development for a few weeks and then suddenly all her development happens on a motor level, while language appears to take a back seat.

Of course, development is not as cut and dried as that. In reality the development of various skills overlap and different components of the same skill are developed at the same time. But it is true to say that development forges ahead in one area at a certain time, while later on another area progresses more rapidly.

The other reason for development taking place in spurts is that the brain needs to consolidate acquired skills. Often when it appears that there is nothing new going on in there, the brain is working very hard at consolidating important foundations, in preparation for the next stage of development.

So comparing babies and measuring your baby's success by her achievement of milestones is at best a pointless exercise and can even cause anxiety if viewed too critically.

ENHANCING DEVELOPMENT

We are all born with a genetic code that makes us who we are. This code is sometimes referred to as our **nature**. It is the potential, present at birth, to achieve optimal physical structure and skill. However, if you have the potential for musical brilliance but you're never exposed to a musical instrument, that potential will not be realized or nurtured. So it is **nurture**, or the environment we develop within, that determines the extent to which we fulfil our potential.

A stimulating environment

Much research has been done in the past 50 years on the effect of the environment on intelligence. Studies of orphaned babies institutionalized at a young age show that a sterile, unstimulating environment results in delays in most areas. Even with intensive intervention later on most babies institutionalised for more than two years never reach their full potential. This is due to lack of stimulation in the critical window period when the brain is so fertile (the first three years). Research has also demonstrated the positive effects of a stimulating environment – intensive stimulation brings about an increase in brain cell connections

---

Most often when a baby has a problem her mother is the first to notice the warning signs. Since developmental milestones occur in broad age-bands, being late for one or two milestones is not a reason to worry. Instead we look for a cluster of signs. These signs may be an indication of **developmental delay**:
- Noticeable floppiness from birth or stiffness that has developed
- Sucking problems or other serious feeding problems
- Not turning towards sounds by three months old
- No eye-contact from early on and lack of interest in people
- Not babbling to self or others by eight months
- Never rolled and not crawling by ten months
- Not moving one side of the body like the other, i.e. asymmetry
- Not reaching for and grasping objects by six months
- Extreme fussing that lasts beyond six months

Take your child to your paediatrician for a full developmental check-up if you notice one or more of these signs. If you are still concerned even when told that your child is fine, consider making an appointment with a physiotherapist or occupational therapist who specializes in neuro-developmental therapy – they can interpret a baby's development better than anyone else and can detect problems at a very early age.

Giftedness may also be an issue in some children and truly gifted children do require special handling. It is very unlikely that advanced milestones in the first year will denote giftedness. Most babies who advance rapidly in the first year are completely in line with their peers by eighteen months. Possible signs of giftedness are:
- Significantly advanced milestones in every area of development
- Very early and advanced language development
- A very early grasp of cognitive tasks, such as memory, spatial awareness and cause and effect.

and enhanced development in the stimulated areas.

Of course most parents want to help their baby reach her full potential, and research such as this reinforces our attempts to enhance our baby's development. Since the 1980s a strong focus on stimulation has emerged and 'stimulation activities' became the buzzwords of childcare as we moved from the 20th to the 21st century. You can buy a multitude of books, read any number of articles in magazines, buy wonderful toys and enrol your baby in classes – all with the aim of enhancing development through stimulation. This frenzied focus on stimulation is motivated by the principle of 'the more, the better'.

Stimulation taken too far

As often happens with good ideas, the idea of baby stimulation can be taken too far. There are many good reasons why stimulation is not a case of 'the more, the better'. Although stimulation improves development in many areas, your baby's emotional development may suffer if stimulation is the primary focus of your interactions with her. This happens when all the activities and stimuli-laden environments overload your baby. Instead of being allowed to spend time in the Calm-Alert state, she receives too much stimulation and can move into an Active-Alert or even a Crying state. This is especially likely if you are not tuned in to her state and misread her signals (see page 32).

An important milestone in emotional development is developing the ability to self-calm. To learn how to self-calm, your baby must recognize her own warning signs of over-stimulation. Then, when she is approaching over-stimulation, she must self-calm and avert a state of overload. Frequently when a baby is stimulated too much she does not develop this independence. Furthermore babies who are constantly exposed to stimuli, often don't develop the ability to play independently or explore their environment at their own pace.

A balanced approach

As already over-burdened parents are beginning to count the cost of pressure to provide their baby with optimal stimulation by way of baby classes and state-of-the-art toys, books are starting to emerge on the market showing the pitfalls of pushing and constantly stimulating babies. Babies whose days are filled with stimulation programmes, both in and out of the home, run the risk of over-stimulation and may show a higher degree of fussing.

There are three key principles when looking for a balanced approach to stimulation:

TAP INTO YOUR BABY'S NATURAL DESIRE TO MASTER HER WORLD

All babies seek to master their world and engage in activity with great enthusi-asm. Instead of subscribing to the frenzy for stimulation, follow a more balanced approach recommended by pioneers in the field of sensory integration: trust your baby's natural desire to develop and master her world and provide an en-riched environment in which she can do so.

PROVIDE A FERTILE ENVIRONMENT

You can enhance your baby's development in all areas by structuring her en-vironment and providing opportunities for constructive, age-appropriate play, taking care not to over-stimulate her, or involve her in too many programmes. By providing a fertile environment for development, you will create the oppor-tunities for her to develop to her full potential on her own without the risk of pushing her too hard.

ACT AS FACILITATOR

Your role in enhancing learning and development, becomes one of facilitator: helping your baby stay in the Calm-Alert state – the state in which she benefits most from her learning opportunities – while setting up or structuring a fertile environment. Done correctly, this will enhance both her emotional and physical development.

BABY-STIMULATION CLASSES

The desire to do the best for our babies puts us under pressure to make use of every opportunity to enhance their development. Baby-stimulation classes offer such an opportunity and you need to weigh up the pros and the cons of the classes in your area.

Benefits of stimulation classes include enhancing specific areas of devel-opment, giving you ideas for games to play with your baby, meeting other moms and babies, and most importantly, spending focused one-on-one time with your baby. But you need to be sensible about when you schedule these classes and whether your baby will benefit from them. Your baby will not benefit from the class if she is being stimulated when she is hungry or tired. Furthermore, some babies, especially very alert and somewhat fussy babies, become over-stimulated by the experience and there is little or no benefit derived from the class.

Don't be pressurized by maternal guilt to attend classes. But if you have the time and means and can be sensible about how it fits into your baby's routine, attend the classes and enjoy the individual, uninterrupted time with your baby.

A sensory diet to enhance development

André's mom put her career on hold to be at home with her first baby. Having made that decision, she feels pressurized to produce a bright, cute and good baby. Constantly reading baby-care books and magazines, she is following André's development with interest. She is powerfully motivated to help André reach his full potential by stimulating his development as much as possible.

Using a sensible, balanced approach, you can do much to help your baby develop to his full potential by interacting with him at the right time and in the right way. Your role is to help your baby experience his world by using his senses, and to provide a sensory diet that will enhance his development.

TOUCH

Babies who are not touched at all after birth (for instance in conditions of extreme deprivation in orphanages) can fail to thrive, and become mentally retarded or even die. The sense of touch is vital for learning and emotional, intellectual and physical development.

Touch is the foundation for the development of perceptual skills such as spatial awareness (body position). As your baby learns about his body through touch, he develops a spatial scheme of himself and eventually the world around him. This body awareness is also very important for learning to move and plan complex movements later on. You may find it difficult to believe, but stimulating your baby's sense of touch will help him learn to ride a bicycle later.

Finally, touch plays a key role in your child's emotional tone, how he socializes and later his ability to concentrate in class and sit still for long enough to complete a task.

Touch in your baby's routine

Incorporate touch into your baby's routine from the very first day by using your own body to touch and massage him. Premature babies in particular benefit tremendously from containing, still touch and especially from 'kangaroo care' (see page 76). Baby massage is a wonderful experience for both you and your baby, and you can start when he is very young.

Babies massaged daily have been shown to have better results in intelligence tests. They also bond with their mother in a way that advances emotional development. Read your baby's signals and watch the awake time to ensure that massaging your baby is a positive experience for both of you. In later months, exposing your baby to a variety of touch experiences in the environment helps him to explore his sense of touch.

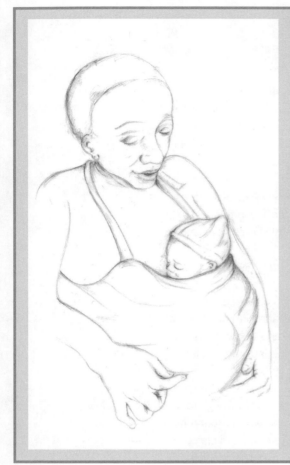

KANGAROO CARE

Kangaroo care has become accepted in most hospitals as a supplementary form of care for premature babies. It entails placing the baby, naked except for a nappy and a hat, in an upright position on his mother's or father's chest with skin-to-skin contact. The baby is bound onto the parent's chest and the parent wears a loose shirt or light covering over the baby. In this way the baby is incubated to maintain a constant temperature.

Benefits to the baby: All babies thrive on touch and it has been found that premature babies gain weight faster and have fewer periods of irregular breathing, fewer bronchial infections and fewer gastric complications if they are nurtured kangaroo style. Kangaroo care maintains the baby's heat supply and temperature control. It promotes energy conservation to allow more frequent Calm-Alert states, sleep and rest periods, and fewer periods of crying.

Benefits to the mother: It empowers her to take an active role in the care of her premature baby. It promotes the bonding process between mother and baby, and it increases the secretion of maternal hormones to enhance production of breast milk.

MOVEMENT

Newborns love the feeling of movement. Rhythmical movement with few changes, such as rocking or being carried, calms them. On the other hand movement that is quick or involves changes in position is alerting and can be used to shift a drowsy baby into a Calm-Alert state. Stimulation of the sense of movement enhances muscle tone and develops motor foundations such as balance and coordination. Through movement your baby learns about his body and the world. It is an important foundation for movement skills and dexterity.

Movement in your baby's routine

The best place for your baby while he's awake, is playing on the floor, or being carried by you. Use a baby sling or pouch for periods when your baby is awake and you need your hands free for chores such as shopping, gardening, writing and so on. Research indicates that babies who are carried in a baby sling or pouch fuss significantly less than others (see page 76). Baby carriers give the sensory input of gentle movement and calming deep touch, neutral warmth and your smell. All these sensory experiences are soothing and will decrease fussing. Even an older baby benefits from being held close to his mom or dad.

Use a baby seat for transportation only. Baby seats do not encourage active movement and babies left in seats for prolonged periods of time do not develop the muscles necessary for rolling and crawling as soon as those babies who only sit in baby seats for transportation. Prams can be useful and do provide some movement stimulation and can be used as a calming tool.

When your baby is older, use both yourself and movement toys such as swings and other everyday objects to either stimulate or calm your baby.

SMELL

The sterile world a baby is born into is very different from the calming environment he's come from. The smells are all new and many are quite clinical. The sense of smell differs from all other senses in that it has direct connections to the emotion centre of the brain. The fact that the sense of smell is so integrally linked to emotion – and thus can be calming – is a good reason for keeping the smells surrounding your baby as calming as possible in the early days.

Smell in your baby's routine
In the early days your baby will spend most of his time close to you. This is beneficial because your smell and the smell of colostrum (early breast milk) are very neutral and calming stimuli. Breast-fed babies have the advantage of having to be held close to feed, so to enjoy this benefit bottle-fed babies should also be held close to the skin for every feed. Your familiar smell will have a calming effect on your baby, should he be struggling to adjust to his new sensory environment.

From quite early on, a security object such as a soft toy or blanket that smells of you and your baby himself has a calming effect. A familiar smell in the cot from early on helps to establish good sleep habits.

SIGHT

Your baby's sight is relatively poorly developed at birth, so this is an area where you should encourage development from early on. For the first few months babies prefer looking at geometric lines and strong colour contrasts and, best of all, faces.

Sight in your baby's routine
Initially your baby's eyes will be very sensitive to light, so to encourage visual attention keep the light level in the room dimmed or muted. Not having to screw

up his eyes against the light will make it easier for your baby to participate in social interaction.

To encourage focus, use visually interesting stimuli such as a black-and-white mobile or a simple picture of a face. Bright colours are stimulating, so keep them for periods of stimulation only. When you want to calm your baby, use dim light or darkness and muted colours.

HEARING

Hearing is intricately linked to language and stimulating this sense is essential for language development. Your newborn baby can hear well, but soon needs to learn to interpret the sounds he hears, for instance where they are coming from, who is speaking, the tone that is used and, finally, what the actual words mean.

Sound in your baby's routine

White noise and rhythmical sounds are calming for a small baby while fast, loud, irregular sounds may over-stimulate him and make him fussy and irritable. Speak to your baby with a slightly high-pitched voice, commonly called 'parentese'. It will encourage him to listen. Use repetition and talk *to* your baby, not just *around* him. Make eye contact and encourage conversations.

APPROPRIATE SENSORY INPUT

Just as the body needs food to grow and develop, so the brain needs sensory input to develop optimally. But stimulating your baby inappropriately for all his waking hours would have as much of an adverse effect on his development as a bowl of porridge for every meal of the day would have on his physical growth. Just like the digestive system requires a balanced diet and time to digest food between meals, your baby can only benefit optimally from stimulation when it is balanced, varied and meaningful, and occurs at a time when he can best respond to the sensory input.

We've seen that the Calm-Alert state is the state in which babies can benefit most from stimulation. You can use specific sensory input to prolong your baby's Calm-Alert state by watching for signals that indicate his state. When his signals indicate that he is becoming over-stimulated you regulate the environment to help him calm down and remain in the Calm-Alert state.

To enhance development we therefore use a sensory diet – a varied and meaningful diet of appropriate sensory input designed to keep a baby calm but also stimulated. The sensory diet we recommend focuses on **Timing, Environment, Activities and Toys** (TEAT) for each age band and each area of development. Since a teat delivers milk to a baby in the first year, the acronym TEAT is particularly appropriate as the framework for a sensory diet that will help your baby to make the most of his world.

Timing

We eat at certain times of the day and not every meal is the same. For instance, we enjoy cornflakes at 8 am, but not at dinner time. Likewise some people like a big breakfast while others prefer a light snack on waking and eat again two hours later. The principle is that we are individuals and our diets differ and the time of day when we take in food changes according to our mood and hunger levels. Appropriate times for your baby's sensory diet are just as important and at certain times of the day your baby may seek more interaction and stimulation than at others.

Time sensory experiences that are intended to enhance development according to the following:

YOUR BABY'S STATE

The optimal time for stimulation is when your baby is in the Calm-Alert state. Instead of arbitrarily imposing stimulation strictly by the clock, for example an hour under the play gym at 11:00 am, choose the timing of the sensory input according to your baby's state.

At certain times of the day a stimulatory 'meal' of movement input will be appropriate, whereas at other times you should keep stimulation to a minimum and rather introduce calming 'snacks'. For instance, keep visual stimulation to a minimum at night when your baby should be sleeping. But during his Calm-Alert state in the afternoon, his visual development would be suitably enhanced by activities such as watching bubbles drift around him, which encourages eye tracking. Watch your baby's state and time activities according to his state. Always be aware of his age-appropriate capacity for being awake (see awake times page 48).

ACTIVITIES IN THE DAY

Your normal daily routine will easily accommodate a variety of stimulating and calming input. By linking the elements of your baby's sensory diet to certain events in the day, it becomes easy to enhance development without having to schedule stimulation time.

- **Nappy-change time** is a good time to introduce visual stimulation (unless it is at night), as your baby will be lying on his back, looking around him, ready to take in some stimulation.
- During **awake time** a walk in the park is good for movement stimulation, you can push him in his pram, carry him on you in a sling, or even give him a gentle push in a swing.
- Daytime **feeds** are an ideal time to stimulate his sense of sound – this you can do by quietly singing to him whilst you are feeding him.
- **Bath time** just before bedtime is a good time to hold back on stimulation and rather use calming input to prepare your baby for the night ahead.

Environment

The nervous system is like a sponge, taking in sensory information all the time. Unlike the mature brain which can filter out excessive or irrelevant sensory information, the young baby's immature nervous system takes it all in. So it stands to reason that the environment will have a major impact on your baby's development. Picture these scenarios:

If your baby is very tired, a busy shopping centre can easily over-stimulate him. He will become irritable and end up crying and not benefit from the experience at all. But if you take him out while he is in a Calm-Alert state, he may welcome the movement stimulation of being carried in a pouch around the shops, and enjoy social interaction with doting grannies who comment on how cute he is.

If you have no option but to shop when your baby is tired or it is time for his sleep, cover the front of his pram with a cotton blanket or towelling nappy. Offer him a dummy to suck and he may drift off to sleep lulled by the white noise around him.

When calm and receptive, your baby will cope well with and, in fact, benefit from, a stimulating environment. But if he is tired or fussing, it would be better to move to a calming environment to help him shift down to his comfort zone, which may be from a state of drowsiness to sleep or from a state of fussing to a Calm-Alert state. Regulating your baby's environment with either calming or stimulating input, as appropriate, is the key to keeping him calm and contented while enhancing his development.

Activities

The games you play and your interactions with your baby affect specific aspects of development. They can be either stimulatory or calming. Implement the activities at the appropriate time and within the appropriate environment to enhance development.

André's mom understands the difference between calming and stimulating sensory input. When she sees André is fussing, she takes him into the nursery, draws the curtains and uses calming motion, such as linear swaying (side-to-side or front-to-back) to calm him down. When the conditions are right for André to be stimulated, his mom plays 'This is the way the lady rides' by gently jogging him up and down on her knee. This develops André's sense of movement and his motor skills. His mom regulates his environment and uses activities at the right time to enhance development.

Most baby magazines have articles on enhancing development in every issue. They are an excellent source of ideas for stimulation activities, as are baby stimulation classes. Watch out for your baby's signals telling you which state he's in, and choose activities accordingly.

Toys

A toy is any object your baby can play with or tool you can use to provide calming or stimulating input. It includes everyday household objects, books, store-bought or home-made toys, music and outdoor equipment. There are wonderful toys on the market for stimulation and even young babies will benefit from appropriate state-of-the-art toys.

Once again it's all a question of timing. Some toys are great for stimulation but should be used only when your baby is ready to benefit from the activity. A busy mobile or activity gym can enhance the development of a three-month-old in many ways as it can promote eye-movement control and eye-hand co-ordination. But trying to interest a tired baby in a mobile or gym is likely to over-stimulate him, pushing him into an overloaded state very quickly. Then he will neither benefit from the activity developmentally nor will he remain calm.

At sleep time an appropriate tool may be a quiet lullaby CD, while just before bath time, when your baby is tired but still has to get through his bath routine calmly before bed, no toys at all may be appropriate.

TEAT FRAMEWORK

When implementing a sensory diet for your baby, you must think about the 'when', 'where', 'how' and 'with what tools'. As a busy mom, remember TEAT - Timing, Environment, Activities and Toys or Tools – as the framework to enhance your baby's development.

In the second part of this book we give you specific, practical suggestions for appropriate stimulation and calming strategies within the six age-bands between birth and one year.

Birth to two weeks

Adjusting to parenthood, especially in the first two weeks of your baby's life, is a daunting process. Coping with the physical after-effects of childbirth, producing adequate breast milk, as well as learning to get by with much less sleep than before, all take their toll on your normal functioning. Especially if you are a first-time parent, you may worry constantly whether what you are doing is absolutely the right thing for your baby. Each new day will present a new set of questions and there will be days when you may feel quite overwhelmed by the responsibility of caring for this little person who has taken over your lives.

FEEDING

You and your baby are just getting to know each other, routines and breast milk supply need time to settle down. So tune in to your baby's signals and your own body. Read this entire section straight through so that you know what to expect. Despite all the excitement, try to relax.

Get breast-feeding off to the right start

The early days of breast-feeding can be a learning curve of note. Most of us have not watched our mothers and sisters breast-feed and acquiring this new skill takes some effort in order to be successful. See page 39 for more information on breast-feeding. Also try these tips:

- Skin to skin – on the day your baby is born, spend time with her naked on your naked chest.
- Latch within the first few hours of birth – the sooner your baby has access to your breasts the better.
- Room in – even if you have chosen for your baby to have her own sleep space, room in for the first few nights so you can respond to her demands for feeds timeously.
- Do not restrict the length of the feeds.
- Let her finish feeding at one breast before offering a feed from the second breast.

Struggling to get it all right in the early days is not unusual, and breast-feeding invariably becomes easier with time. However, if breast-feeding is painful and you are feeling increasingly anxious about feeding, it is a good idea to call on a lactation consultant to assist you to get it right.

Milk supply

In the first two weeks, babies generally feed on demand. If you are breast-feeding, demand feeding at this stage is essential to establish a good milk supply.

Babies are usually quite sleepy for the first 48 hours, as they recover from the birthing process and adjust to their new world. Food reserves from the womb and the colostrum (rich in nutrients and antibodies) from your breast milk in the first few days after birth are more than adequate to satisfy your baby's nutritional needs. Once your milk comes in, on day three (or thereabouts), your body will adjust the supply to the demands of your baby. You are producing enough milk if your baby has at least six wet nappies a day, is generally feeding two- to four-hourly and is content and sleepy between feeds.

Your baby may lose up to 10% of her birth weight in the first few days, but should regain her birth weight by the time she is two weeks old.

Learn to read your baby's signals

Although demand breast-feeding is important initially to establish a good milk supply, it is equally important to learn to interpret your baby's signals indicating her state (see page 32), so that you can allow her the opportunity to learn to self-calm before you assume that she needs a feed. During this period you are just getting to know each other and whilst some days will be easy, others may be difficult. Not understanding your newborn's cries, you may resort to feeding her whenever she cries. Instead, make a special effort to read her signals and to consider her sensory needs along with her need for food, shelter and warmth.

Frequency of feeds

Breast milk is digested more quickly than formula, therefore breast-fed babies initially need more frequent feeding than babies on formula milk.

If you are breast-feeding and your baby is thriving, try to feed no more frequently than two-hourly. As your baby's suck becomes stronger and your milk supply improves, the period between feeds may become longer (three- to four-hourly). If she is on formula milk, initially feed her three-hourly. If she is fussing when it is not time for a feed, use other calming strategies (see page 62).

Don't let your baby sleep longer than four hours without a feed during the day – wake her up. But as long as she is gaining weight and was not premature, leave her to wake you after her last evening feed.

Your diet while breast-feeding

Your body needs a huge amount of energy to produce enough milk for your baby for 24 hours. You use as much energy to do this as you do to run a half-marathon. To provide you with the necessary energy it is essential to follow a diet high in both carbohydrates (rice, pasta, potatoes) and protein (meat, dairy, eggs, fish, legumes). You also have to drink plenty of fluids (at least two litres a day) and eat a variety of fruit and vegetables.

There are many theories and old wives tales about what you should and what you should not eat while breast-feeding. The reality is that you should continue with the diet you ate while pregnant, avoiding:
• Alcohol and medication;

- Caffeine, sugars and stimulants, which may cause your baby to become over-stimulated and irritable.

If your baby is unusually fussy, experiment with avoiding the following and see if it makes a difference to her mood:
- Onions, cabbage and beans and other foods that produce wind;
- Dairy products if you think that your baby may have a lactose sensitivity (see page 57);
- Excessive intake of Vitamin B12, which may lead to decreased milk supply.

SUPPLEMENTS WHILE BREAST-FEEDING

As you muddle along during these first two weeks, adjusting to parenthood, you may not be eating a balanced diet. Snatched meals of convenience food or take-outs do not provide the essential nutrients your body needs to produce milk. Consider taking supplements high in lucerne and alfalfa protein, with the right amount of vitamin B. These are available in tablet form or as a tea. A tonic made from blackthorn berries is a refreshing and energizing drink mixed with a little water or as an ingredient of Jungle Juice. You can drink two litres a day to enhance milk production.

Jungle Juice
50 ml blackthorn berry tonic (Schlehen elixir)
1 litre apple, berry or grape juice
2 litres water
1 sachet fruit-flavoured Rehydrat solution
1 Cal-C-Vita tablet and a few drops of Rescue Remedy to help you relax (optional)

Note: If you suffer from recurrent fungal infections such as thrush (*Candida albicans*), replace the fruit juice with water to reduce the sugar content.
(With thanks to the Natural Health Association of South Africa)

SLEEP

At this stage, you can expect your baby to sleep most of the time. She is not likely to stay awake happily for longer than 40 to 60 minutes before needing to go back to sleep. You will need to help her differentiate between day and night.
- Separate day and night with a routine bath at the same time each evening. At this time, limit stimulation and ensure a calm environment (closed curtains, calming music, limited eye-contact and talking). At night, after the last evening feed, allow her to wake up for the next feed by herself, provided that she is gaining weight and she was not premature. Night feeds should be strictly business, in very dim light and with no eye-contact, talking or stimulation.
- At the first morning feed, greet her happily, open the curtains and provide some stimulation. During the day, stimulate her appropriately during her 40 to 60 minutes of awake time to let her know that this is her social, wakeful time.

Try to be in tune with her signals and respond accordingly. Don't let her sleep for longer than four hours at a stretch during the day and wake her if necessary for her feed. Limit outings, especially to crowded and noisy places. Try to keep her at home and in her calm sleep space for sleeps.

FLEXIBLE ROUTINE FOR BIRTH TO TWO WEEKS

- Your baby will be feeding two- to three-hourly during the day.
- Night feeds may become progressively less frequent and she may start to stretch for four to five hours between feeds.
- Provided she is gaining weight, do not offer a feed if she is crying or fussing less than two hours since the last feed. Rather encourage self-calming by non-nutritive sucking or calm her with rocking or swaddling.
- Limit her awake time to 40 to 60 minutes (between one sleep and the next) and plan your care-giving, outings and stimulation within this time.
- She should be sleeping for a large part of her day, approximately 18 to 20 hours in a 24-hour cycle.

WHAT'S BABY UP TO?

In the early weeks your baby is predominantly in a flexed position, with her legs tucked up towards her stomach, similar to the curled-up position of the last few months in the womb. This **flexion** helps her to feel organized because it's so stable. This is why, for a long time, your baby will pull back into flexion when she gets a fright. Your baby's first motor (movement) task is to uncurl by strengthening her back muscles to extend or stretch her out. Her neck muscles are very weak and it is important that they strengthen to hold up her head.

Primitive reflexes

In the early weeks, primitive reflexes control your baby's movements. The **grasp reflex** keeps her hands clasped most of the time. The **Moro reflex** is elicited in response to the head falling backwards and results in the hands clasping into

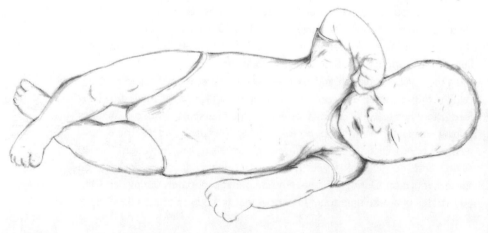

fists and the arms flying out and then in. Touching your baby's cheek next to her mouth stimulates the **rooting reflex** which will cause her to turn her head in that direction. This reflex is important for feeding, as is the **sucking reflex**.

When she turns her head to one side, the **ATNR** or **fencing reflex** causes the arm and leg on that side to stretch out (see illustration below left). This reflex is vital for the start of eye-hand co-ordination as it allows your baby to see her hand. At this stage she can focus on objects about 20 cm away (close to her arm's length). During this period, all these reflexes affect your baby's movement so there is very little voluntary movement.

Social beginnings

Your newborn spends a lot of time sleeping, but over the next two weeks the drowsiness will give way to a somewhat more alert state. Just after she's born, before going into a Drowsy state, your baby will spend some time in the Calm-Alert state, getting to know her mom and dad. When she is in this state, she may make tongue and mouth movements to imitate talking. Even from her first day your little bundle is a social creature. She will recognize caregivers by smell by the end of the first day, by voice in the next few days and by sight by the end of the first week.

ENHANCING DEVELOPMENT

The newborn's brain cannot yet inhibit or shut out excess sensory stimuli, which is why many young babies become over-stimulated and at around 10 days to two weeks some start having prolonged periods of crying, commonly known as colic. Following your baby's cues, you will be able to pre-empt crying by removing her from stimuli as soon as she shows signs of irritability or fussiness.

In the early days and right up to about three months of age it falls to you to regulate sensory input for your baby. The first step is to determine what over-stimulates your baby and how to calm her. Each baby is unique in the amount of sensory stimuli she can handle. At this stage the combination of a little stimulation and a lot of calming is the secret.

Your baby's head is very heavy relative to the rest of her body and her first important motor task is to strengthen her neck and back muscles.

A sensory diet

We do not advocate many stimulation activities at this early stage since the early days are overwhelming enough for parents and baby. Focus on keeping your baby's world as calming as possible while establishing breast-feeding or getting a good bottle-feeding routine under way.

ENVIRONMENT

At this stage a calm environment is the secret of a calm baby. Try to imitate the calm world from which your baby has just emerged as much as possible.

SIGHT	• Use soft, muted or neutral colours in the nursery. Keep the lights low so that you can take your baby to a room that is visually calming when she is fussing. • Keep new faces to a minimum, limiting visitors in the first few weeks.
HEARING	• Soft sounds and white noise are the most calming sensory input for your baby. • Avoid very noisy environments as much as possible in the early days. She may not fuss at the time but later you may have to deal with a fussy baby.
TOUCH	• Deep-touch pressure and touch to the back are calming. • Ensure that scratchy fabrics, such as labels and lace, are not touching your baby's skin.
MOVEMENT	• Use slow rocking and rhythmical movements to calm her. • Avoid erratic and unpredictable movements.
SMELL	• Non-distinct smells are better than pungent odours. • During the first six weeks do not to wear perfume or after-shave lotion. Your own body smell is the most wonderful perfume in the world to your little one. Also ask grannies not to wear perfume for the early visits. • Wash your baby's clothes in odourless detergent. • Use a tablespoon of vinegar as an odourless fabric softener.

ROUTINE-RELATED ACTIVITIES (TIMING)

Make both stimulating activities and calming strategies part of your daily care-giving programme.

SLEEP TIME

A quiet, calm sleep environment is essential at every stage.

SIGHT	• A visually calming room is vital for sleep. Use curtains with block-out lining to teach your baby that dark time is sleep time, and a light dimmer for night feeds.
HEARING	• White noise is particularly calming and will help your baby fall asleep. Record the sound of the vacuum cleaner or washing machine or buy CDs of white noise.

TOUCH	• Swaddle your baby before she goes to sleep to provide deep-touch pressure and to prevent her arms from jerking and waking her up if she startles in her sleep. • Keep your baby at a constant comfortable temperature with suitable covering.
MOVEMENT	• Rock your baby to calm her **before** sleep.
MOTOR development	• Put your baby to sleep on her side – this is a better position for muscle development than lying her flat on her back. Place a rolled towel next to her so she can't roll onto her tummy. Sleeping on the stomach has been associated with cot deaths (SIDS).
SMELL	• Place a piece of clothing that smells of you into the cot with her.

NAPPY CHANGE TIME

When you are changing your baby's nappy she is usually awake and alert (except at night feeds) which make it a good time for her to focus on something.

SIGHT	• Show your baby black-and-white pictures and mobiles during daytime nappy changes to encourage focus.
HEARING	• Talk quietly to your baby using 'parentese', which encourages her to concentrate on your voice.
TOUCH	• Use gentle but firm touch when changing her nappy.

BATH TIME

First baths can be frightening, so use soothing sensory input. This is a great time for touch activities, as it is one of the few times during her day that your baby is naked.

HEARING	• Your baby's first few baths are a very new experience for her. Make her feel secure by using your voice to calm her.
TOUCH	• Use a calming touch to lightly massage her whole body. Babies who are lovingly touched every day thrive. • If your baby is fractious in the bath, bath her swaddled in a thin muslin cloth or place a small face cloth on her tummy.

SENSE-ABLE SECRET
Bath time should be the start of the bedtime routine, so don't over-excite your baby at this time of day. Play quietly and then be very calm after the bath.

Motor development	• Let her kick in the bath and stretch out her curled-up legs. Support her head as her neck muscles cannot yet do so.
Smell	• Use fragrance-free products in the bath.

Awake time

In the early days your baby spends very little time awake, other than feed time. Interact with your baby but don't over-stimulate her in these precious few wakeful moments.

Sight	• To encourage focusing, place objects 20-25 cm from your baby's face. • Animate your face when you speak to her and let her see your mouth. Wear lipstick to help her focus on your mouth. • Your face and soothing voice will also calm your baby.
Hearing	• Your voice is one of the most calming sounds to your baby. Talk in soft crooning tones and sing softly to her.
Touch	• Handle your baby firmly but gently and support her head. • Hold her tightly when she's crying and rub or pat her back. • Limit the unfamiliar, unpredictable touch of visitors. • Incorporate baby massage into your routine as soon as it seems manageable.
Movement	• Carrying your baby in a sling best mimics the containing environment of the womb. • Don't be tempted to play with her too roughly. Quick moving or lifting is overwhelming for your baby's immature nervous system.
Motor development	• Place her on her tummy a few times a day when she is in the Calm-Alert state so she can practise lifting her head. • Place her on her tummy on top of your stomach when you are lying back. Talk to her to encourage her to lift her head a little.

Travelling time

Protect your baby from the overwhelming sensory environment outside her room by regulating sensory input.

Sight	• When out and about, cover the front of the pram or baby chair with a nappy or blanket to keep bright lights and excessive visual stimulation to a minimum.
Hearing	• Play soothing baroque music when you travel by car.
Movement	• A ride in a pram or in a pouch or sling helps calm your baby.

FEED TIME

Quiet, soothing input will keep your baby calm to focus on feeding.

Touch	• If your baby is too drowsy to feed well, stroke her cheek with your finger or damp cotton wool, or occasionally tickle her feet.
Hearing	• Talk or read to your baby while she feeds, unless it distracts her, causing her to fuss.

TOYS AND TOOLS

You are your baby's best toy and you need not buy anything else. But if you are investing in toys, here are some ideas for suitable toys you can buy or make.

Sight	• A black-and-white mobile. • Cut out a picture of a baby's face from a magazine and put it next to the changing mat or in her car seat for her to focus on.
Hearing	• A CD of soft baroque and other classical music. • Commercially available CDs of womb sounds, heartbeat and dolphin sounds are all excellent for calming.

BABY MASSAGE

Touch is one of the most powerful mediums that you can use to bond with your baby. Baby massage is a wonderful experience for both you and your baby and can begin within days of your baby's birth.

In the 5th century BC Hippocrates said, "The way to health is to have a scented bath and an oiled massage each day". General physiological benefits of massage include improved respiration, better lymph and blood circulation and improved gastro-intestinal function. For babies it has many specific benefits:

• Deep touch and massage calm your baby and are therefore excellent remedies for colic.

- Massage speeds up the progress of premature and low birth-weight babies.
- Babies who are regularly massaged are less likely to cry excessively, they sleep better and gain weight faster.
- It is calming and a wonderful way to develop body awareness which is essential for the development of spatial perception later. This in turn is vital for academic skills, such as writing and maths.

Guidelines

For both you and your baby to derive the most benefit from a massage session, you need to follow some basic guidelines:

- Babies respond well to routine, so try to schedule massage at the same time every day. Ensure that your baby is in the Calm-Alert state – the state in which she is most responsive.
- Keep the massage environment calming and free from distractions for you and your baby.
- Make sure your nails are short and remove all jewellery. Warm your hands beforehand.
- Have a change of baby clothes at hand so that you can dress your baby without having to get up when the massage is over.
- Once your baby is older it will be useful to have a small manipulative toy at hand to occupy her if need be during massage.

Giving a baby massage

Position yourself comfortably in a warm spot out of draughts, leaning against a wall or pile of cushions. Undress your baby completely. Put her on a towel or nappy in case of mishaps. You can place the towel in the tumble dryer to warm it before you begin the massage. Mix three to five drops of lavender or camomile essential oil with about 20 ml of a carrier oil such as almond, grape seed or extra virgin olive oil. Put a little of this in the palm of your hand to warm it up – use just enough to allow your hands to move smoothly over your baby's skin. Now proceed as follows:

HEAD

Gently hold your baby's face and quietly tell her that you'll be touching her. Move your fingers round her head, while supporting it, and massage the scalp in tiny circles. Move your hands down her neck to her shoulders in a stroking movement.

LEGS

Make contact by placing your hands on her hips for a moment.
Gliding stroke – grasp the hip of one leg in both hands and stroke the leg towards the toes with both hands. Repeat by letting go and moving one hand at a time back to the hip. Repeat three times on each leg.

FEET
Thumb press – apply firm pressure to the bottom of the foot for three seconds, using the pad of your thumb.

TOES
Toe squeeze – gently squeeze each toe individually from the base of the toe to its tip. Use the same action as for fingers.

CHEST
Shoulder to toes – place your hands on both shoulders simultaneously and glide both hands down her body to her toes. Bring one hand back to one shoulder, then the other hand. Repeat.

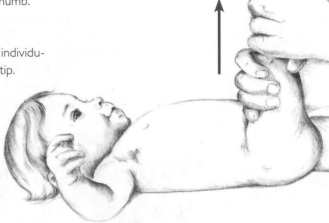

TUMMY
Always move your hands in a clockwise direction – the direction of the intestines. Choose one of the following strokes which are all excellent for babies with colic and other digestive problems such as elimination difficulties.

   Gentle pressure – begin with this stroke to alert your baby to where you are touching. Just place your hand on her tummy, maintaining this point of contact for a moment.

   Paddle wheel – place one hand just under her ribs and glide your hand towards her groin area. Before lifting your hand, place your other hand under her rib cage and repeat. Continue alternating hands, making sure one is always in touch with her skin.

   Sun and moon – this stroke needs practice to get co-ordinated. Your left hand moves in a continuous clockwise circle (sun). Your right hand moves in an arc from your left (9 o'clock) to your right (5 o'clock). The arc begins when your left hand is closest to her groin (6 o'clock).

   I love you – accompany this three-part stroke with the words "I love you". (I) Place your dominant hand below her rib cage on your right (baby's left side) and stroke down making an 'I'. (Love) Move your hand to the other side of your baby's rib cage, glide it across the top of her tummy, under her chest and then down to her groin. This forms an upside-down 'L'. (You) Place your hand near your baby's right hip (your left), stroke up to her rib cage, then across, then down the opposite side, making an upside-down 'U'.

   Finish with gentle pressure.

ARMS

Gliding stroke – place your hands at the top of the shoulder and stroke the arm towards the hand. Repeat by letting go and moving one hand at a time back to the shoulder. Repeat this stroke three times on each arm.

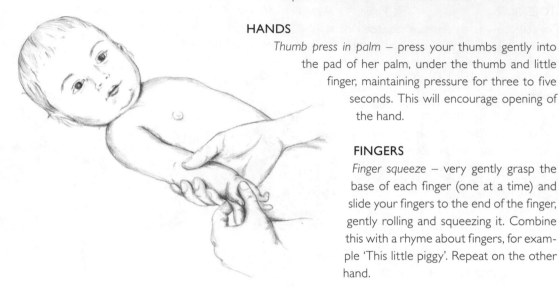

HANDS

Thumb press in palm – press your thumbs gently into the pad of her palm, under the thumb and little finger, maintaining pressure for three to five seconds. This will encourage opening of the hand.

FINGERS

Finger squeeze – very gently grasp the base of each finger (one at a time) and slide your fingers to the end of the finger, gently rolling and squeezing it. Combine this with a rhyme about fingers, for example 'This little piggy'. Repeat on the other hand.

BACK

Turn your baby over onto her tummy, on the mat or on your lap.

Swoop down back – gently stroke down her back from her neck to her buttocks. For a small baby, use one hand, resting the other one on the buttocks. For a bigger baby, use both hands simultaneously on either side of the back.

Finish with a cuddle.

CAUTION

- Do not massage your baby for a few days after immunizations, as her temperature may be slightly raised.
- At all times keep your baby's joints well aligned to prevent damage to the joints. Always use firm but gentle strokes.
- Be attuned to your baby's signals after a massage. If she is unusually irritable, wait for a few weeks before doing another massage.

Two to six weeks

You'll soon be a month into the adventure of parenthood. Days that fly by (and nights that don't) probably seem to be a way of life now, ruled by this tiny bundle weighing no more than a small puppy. You'll slowly be learning to read your baby's signals and you'll have a clearer understanding of his needs. But it's quite normal to still have bouts of anxiety about his well-being – particularly with regards to feeding and sleeping.

FEEDING

Your baby will most likely be settling down into a feeding routine, but there may be some temporary hiccups, especially during growth spurts. In general you'll be getting to know your baby's hunger pattern and, if you are sensitive to his signals, you probably won't have evening fussing to deal with.

Milk supply

Your baby should have regained his birth weight by now. If he continues gaining weight and is generally happy and content to feed two- to four-hourly, you can be sure that your milk supply is adequate. Check that he is having at least six wet nappies a day. Ensure that you keep up an adequate supply of breast milk by drinking plenty of fluids and increasing your protein and carbohydrate intake.

If you are bottle-feeding, stick to the guidelines on page 44 to determine how much milk he needs.

Growth spurts

A growth spurt is quite common at around the four-week mark. Your baby may be extra fussy and only settle if fed. He may demand as much as two-hourly feeding and may wake more frequently than before at night. This is quite normal. But before automatically assuming that he is hungry, try other calming strategies. Should these not work, you can assume he is experiencing a growth spurt. Feed him accordingly.

Fussiness caused by growth spurts should settle within 24 to 48 hours when your baby's feeding schedule should return to its previous pattern. If fussing persists, go through the process of elimination (see page 56).

Supplementary or 'top-up' feeding

'Top-up' feeds (see page 45) should not be necessary if your baby is feeding two- to four-hourly during the day, stretching for four to five hours between feeds at night, is gaining weight and is generally happy and content. But these feeds may sometimes be necessary during a growth spurt.

Frequency of feeds

Generally, if your baby is healthy and thriving, don't offer him a feed if he is fussy less than three hours since the last feed. Offer him other methods of calming (see page 64).

Provided he has regained his birth weight, and continues to grow, he can be fed three- to four-hourly during the day. After the last evening feed at about 7 pm, provided he is gaining weight, wait for him to wake you up for a feed. He may sleep four to six hours without needing a feed during the night.

Some babies like to 'cluster-feed' (feed one- to two-hourly) in the late afternoon or early evening. This builds up a stockpile of energy to carry them through for longer periods without food during the night. But only cluster-feed if you are sure that he is hungry.

Most evening fussiness is due to over-tiredness and sensory overload, which are common at this time of day. Explore other methods of calming first. Overfeeding can cause winds and discomfort, commonly misinterpreted as hunger or colic.

NAPPY RASH

Fussing may be the result of discomfort caused by nappy rash. Change nappies frequently and clean your baby's genital and anal area thoroughly at each change. Avoid perfumed or alcohol-based wipes and apply a topical protective cream to the nappy area before putting on a clean nappy. Make sure that cloth nappies are rinsed well. Most nappy rashes are a simple dermatitis caused by ammonia in urine and faeces. Some nappy rashes are caused by thrush and need to be treated with an anti-fungal cream.

If your baby is premature, take great care when using disposable nappies. Premature babies have less collagen in their skin, increasing the risk of blister formation and skin damage should the adhesive tape on disposable nappies stick to their skin.

SLEEP

Your baby's awake time should be no more than 60 minutes at a stretch. He will probably still be sleeping for most of the day. Around two weeks of age he may become more alert and difficult to get to sleep. If you do not make an effort to have him sleep regularly, you may find he is irritable and more likely to suffer from colic.

Remember that it is still the duration of the awake time that determines the sleep time, and not the other way round. An over-tired baby will not sleep well. If your baby is still waking more frequently to feed at night than during the day, he may have his day-night rhythms muddled. Use a regular bedtime routine to help him differentiate between day and night (see page 50).

Colic

Your content newborn who fed well and slept for a good deal of the time may suddenly become fractious and irritable during the two-to-six-week period. During this stage, limit fussing by:

- Ruling out physical reasons for crying – if your baby appears listless, fussy and is not drinking enthusiastically take him to your doctor for a check;
- Ensuring he is sleeping regularly during the day by watching his awake times and reading his signals;
- Restricting stimulation and over-handling by numerous people, especially in the early evening when he is more likely to be over-stimulated;
- Keeping him swaddled most of the time (see page 23).

See page 66 for practical tips on handling fussy evenings and colicky patches.

FLEXIBLE ROUTINE FOR TWO TO SIX WEEKS

- Your baby will be feeding two- to four-hourly during the day.
- Provided he is gaining weight, do not offer milk feeds if he is crying or fussing less than three hours since the last feed.
- Expect a growth spurt, lasting about 24 hours, when he is about four weeks old. Feed him two-hourly if necessary.
- Once he is over his growth spurt, stretch his feeds as close to four hours apart as you can by offering him 20 to 40 ml of cooled boiled water.
- If he is unsettled, encourage non-nutritive sucking (hand-to-mouth or dummy), swaddle him in a cotton blanket, give him a massage or gently rock him.
- Limit his awake time to 60 minutes at a stretch and plan your care-giving, outings and stimulation within this time.
- Avoid noisy, crowded environments, but if you have no choice, go there during his awake time.
- He should be sleeping for about 18 to 20 hours in a 24-hour cycle.

WHAT'S BABY UP TO?

Reflexes still predominate, although they will gradually become more integrated over the next few weeks and most will disappear. His arms and legs move a great deal now, especially the arms, which swipe wildly through the air. You'll notice that his hands will be less fisted. He does not yet reach for objects, but stares intently at them, almost reaching out with his eyes.

Uncurling

Your baby is less curled-up, but still needs opportunities to work his back and neck muscles. On his tummy he will start to lift his head off the bed and, when held in a sitting position, he may hold his head upright for a little while. When you pull him into a sitting position from lying on his back, he will start to hold his head in line with his body. By six weeks he will have uncurled considerably, have straighter hips and knees and be able to hold his head up for a few minutes.

Visual acuity

This stage of development is very focused on visual acuity and co-ordinating eye movements. Your baby enjoys patterns of any kind, as well as contrasting colours. He recognizes your face – a firm favourite. He will watch people if they are in his line of vision and even turn his head towards them.

The big milestone that makes all the hard work seem worthwhile is reached around the six-week mark: your baby starts smiling. He responds to your voice, holds your gaze for longer and tries to talk with little throaty noises.

ENHANCING DEVELOPMENT

The big motor goal of this stage is to strengthen the back and neck muscles. This is essential for head control which is important for crawling later on. If your baby does not spend time on his tummy in the early days, he will not be comfortable in this position later when he should be developing his crawling skills. On a fine-motor level his goal is to open his hands and become aware of them.

Try to ensure that most of the day is calming. Only provide stimulation when your baby is in the Calm-Alert state, which will usually be after a meal, but not immediately before he goes to sleep. During this awake period, massage him and provide visual stimulation. Take walks and talk to your baby. Always watch for signs of sensory overload (see page 33).

A sensory diet

At this stage, more than any other, your baby runs the risk of sensory overload. Since he cannot yet control or habituate the amount of sensory stimulation flooding in, he is completely dependent on you to ensure that he does not become over-stimulated. If your baby is colicky, you will have to be extra vigilant to implement calming strategies as opposed to stimulating him.

ENVIRONMENT

Since your baby is so vulnerable to sensory overload, keep his environment predominantly calming.

SIGHT	• He is still very sensitive to visual stimuli, therefore block-out curtains are important to keep his room dark, especially for bedtime.
HEARING	• He loves your voice – speak to him frequently to encourage language development.

TOUCH	• Deep-touch pressure and touch to the back are calming and your baby loves your touch.
MOVEMENT	• He only needs calming movements such as rocking.
MOTOR DEVELOPMENT	• To strengthen his neck muscles, place your baby on his tummy when he's awake. Have a spot in each room where he can lie on his tummy while you are busy in that room.
SMELL	• Keep smells calming and neutral. • Don't wear perfume or aftershave.

ROUTINE-RELATED ACTIVITIES (TIMING)

Make both stimulating activities and calming strategies part of your daily care-giving programme.

SLEEP TIME

A quiet, calm sleep environment remains essential.

SIGHT	• Use curtains with block-out lining and avoid bright lights or colours at sleep time. Use a light dimmer for night feeds. • Do not have a mobile or bright pictures on the wall near his cot or sleep area.
TOUCH	• Continue to swaddle your baby at night and for day sleeps. • If he fusses once you've put him down, place your hand gently but firmly on his back.
MOVEMENT	• Use a rocking chair to rock your baby into a Drowsy state. Put him in his bed before he's fully asleep.
MOTOR DEVELOPMENT	• Sleeping on his side is better for muscle development than lying flat on his back. Alternate the side he sleeps on to allow both sides of his body to develop equally.

CAUTION

Research has shown that when a baby sleeps on his stomach, the risk of sudden infant death syndrome (SIDS) increases.

NAPPY CHANGE TIME

When your baby is lying on his back while you change his nappy, use the time for a bit of stimulation.

SIGHT	• Set up a black-and-white mobile – toy zebras or black-and-white blocks or even a white paper plate with black designs on it. Place it about 20 cm from your baby's face. Until your baby is about four weeks old, hang a long mobile beside his head (changing sides daily) so he can focus on it. This will relax your baby for changing time.
HEARING	• Talk to your baby in a high-pitched voice (parentese).
MOTOR DEVELOPMENT	• From four weeks, hang the mobile above his head to encourage him to keep his head in midline. This will strengthen his neck muscles.

BATH TIME

Bath time is the start of the bedtime routine, so don't over-excite your baby. Rather play quietly and keep things very calm after his bath.

SIGHT	• Holding your baby in the bath puts you at just the right distance to make eye-contact and talk to him.
HEARING	• Play soft classical music or lullabies, especially after his bath and during massage time.
TOUCH	• Warm the room so that your baby is comfortable when naked or being dressed. • Massage your baby's arms, legs and tummy while soaping. • Towel him down with a warm terry towel, using deep-pressure touch.
MOTOR DEVELOPMENT	• Encourage him to kick in the bath, stretching his legs.

TOUCH AVERSION

A tactile defensive baby may not enjoy touch. Watch for signs of irritability in your baby when he is touched. If this is accompanied by extreme fussiness in general, go through the checklist for regulatory and sensory processing disorders (see Appendix A, page 151).

AWAKE TIME

As your baby has slightly more awake time, play with him, taking care not to over-stimulate him.

SIGHT	• Make eye-contact when he is awake or initiates eye contact. Follow his lead if he looks away. • Move a brightly coloured picture book or toy slowly within his line of vision.
HEARING	• Talk to your baby as he lies on your lap so that he learns to turn his head to look at you. This strengthens his neck muscles and develops his listening and visual skills. • Sing lullabies and laugh with your baby.
TOUCH	• Awake time after the morning feed when your baby is in the Calm-Alert state is a good time for a baby massage. • Massage his hands and play finger and hand games with rhymes to make him aware of his hands.
MOVEMENT	• Rhythmical linear movement (rocking from side to side or back to front) is calming. • Sway and even turn around slowly to stimulate the sense of movement during playtime.
MOTOR DEVELOPMENT	• Let your baby lie on his tummy with an interesting object close by to look at so that he will raise his head to strengthen his neck. If your baby falls asleep in this position it is fine if you are nearby and keeping an eye on him. • Lay him on his tummy on your chest. Wanting to look up at your face will encourage him to lift his head. Initially prop yourself up on cushions to decrease the angle at which he has to lift his head.

TRAVELLING TIME

Choose your destinations and the time you spend out and about carefully. Your baby is very susceptible to over-stimulation.

SIGHT	• Continue to cover the front of the pram or baby chair with a nappy or blanket to keep out bright lights and excessive visual stimulation.
TOUCH	• Carry your baby in a sling or pouch facing towards you. Both the deep touch and the movement will be calming for your baby.

FEED TIME

Quiet, soothing input will keep your baby calm to focus on feeding.

SIGHT	• Pin a red ribbon to your bra strap or top to give your baby something to focus on while feeding. This works for both breast- and bottle-fed babies.
HEARING	• Talk to your baby or read to him so that he becomes familiar with language and tone changes in your voice. Using a high-pitched tone is more important than what you say.
MOTOR DEVELOPMENT	• Alternate the side on which you feed.
SMELL	• Don't wear perfume or aftershave.

SENSE-ABLE SECRET *If your baby gets distracted or chokes on the milk when you talk or read to him while he feeds, that stimulation is too much for him. In that case let feed times be quiet times.*

TOYS AND TOOLS

You are still your baby's best toy. But here are some additional ideas.

SIGHT	• Hang a safe baby mirror (commercially available) above your baby to reflect light as it swings. • Make or buy a black-and-white mobile and hang it over the changing mat. • Cut pictures of faces from magazines, stick them on card and put the cards in the car where he can see them or next to him when he's lying down during awake time.
HEARING	• Buy or make a rattle for your baby to listen to and turn towards (he won't be able to hold it yet). • Buy CDs of calming music.

TOUCH	• Make a large texture mat using a variety of fabrics – felt, fake fur, corduroy, denim, silk, cotton. You can even sew on a few buttons or bells (very securely). Let your baby touch the different textures to develop his sense of touch.
MOTOR DEVELOPMENT	• Use the texture mat for tummy and floor time.

Perinatal distress (PND) is more common than most people imagine. Previously known as **post-natal depression**, it has been renamed recently. 'Perinatal' indicates that these feelings may emerge at any time **around** the birth of your baby: during pregnancy, shortly after the birth or as much as 18 months later. The word 'distress' indicates that the feelings are not limited to depression and feeling down but may include simply feeling anxious and distressed about caring for your baby. If you feel:
• Out of control, frustrated and very irritable
• Scared or panicky, anxious and worried, sad or miserable most of the time
• Unable to laugh or to feel joy
• Unable to cope
• Afraid to be alone
• Unusually tearful
• As though you are going crazy

Or if you have:
• Difficulty in sleeping
• No sex drive
• Thoughts about harming yourself or your baby,

you may be suffering from perinatal distress. Please seek help.
Call the PNDSA helpline on 082 882 0072 or go to www.pndsa.org.za.

Six to twelve weeks

Reaching the magical six-week mark is a turning point for most moms. Suddenly all the hard work and lack of sleep seem worthwhile, as your baby begins to reward your efforts with some social interaction.

If your baby is restless and unsettled, and is generally unhappily awake, it is worth going through the process of elimination (see page 56). If you are convinced that you have covered all bases, it might be worthwhile taking a closer look at her sensory world. She might simply be over-tired or over-stimulated or both – and has reached the end of her tether. This is usually the reason why colic sets in, as the constant sensory overload simply becomes too much for her to bear.

Unexplained crying or **colic** is common in many babies under three months of age. It is reassuring to know that this crying peaks at around six weeks, but by 12 weeks of age, almost all colic has abated, and your baby will be more settled and better able to self-soothe.

FEEDING

When your baby is about six to eight weeks old, you will have another **growth spurt** to deal with and you may have concerns about the adequacy of your milk supply. But if you look after your own health and nutrition, your milk supply will be fine.

Growth spurts last for 24-48 hours, so feed your baby more frequently if necessary. Friends and family may try pressurizing you into introducing solids but at this age it is not recommended.

Milk supply

If your baby is stretching the period between feeds from three to four hours during the day, and has a long stretch of six to seven hours at night, is happy and content, gaining weight, and has six wet nappies a day, your milk supply is adequate. But if she remains hungry and unsettled beyond the usual growth spurt, there may be a problem with your milk supply. If so, try one or a combination of the following remedies:
* Drink plenty of extra fluid.
* Try to rest as much as possible.
* Feed your baby two- to three-hourly for 24 hours to stimulate milk supply.
* Speak to your clinic sister about vitamin or herbal supplements for yourself.
* Make yourself some Jungle Juice (see page 85).

If you are bottle-feeding, stick to the guidelines on page 44 to determine how much milk your baby needs.

Dealing with a hungry baby

Your baby should be sleeping for a stretch of around six to seven hours at night without needing milk, and her day feeds should be in the region of every three to four hours. If there is a marked change in her feeding pattern, you may need to re-evaluate her nutritional needs.

- She may just be having a growth spurt, in which case her appetite for more frequent feeds should settle within 48 hours.
- If you are exclusively breast-feeding, accept that she will require more frequent feeding both day and night.
- If you are happy to include supplementary or complementary feeds to help your hungry baby, then do so. Use expressed breast milk or formula milk (see page 46). Ask your health-care provider to recommend a suitable formula milk for this purpose.
- If she is formula fed, consider changing her formula to one for hungry babies.
- Introducing solid food into your baby's diet is not recommended until she is four months old.

SLEEP

By now your baby is settling into a sleeping and feeding pattern. She probably needs three sleeps a day: one long one and two shorter ones. You will find that she tires after 60-80 minutes of being awake. As a rule of thumb, start to prepare her for day sleeps ten minutes before her sleep is due. Swaddle her and take her to a dark room or hold her, gently swaying from side to side, to help her unwind from the stimulation of the awake time. This unwinding before she takes a nap will ensure that she is not over-tired or over-stimulated and that you can put her down **happily awake** to go to sleep. Don't let her have a long sleep if it is less than two hours before bedtime, as she will have difficulty falling asleep in the evening.

Having a regular bed and bath time is now essential. This forms part of setting the stage for sleep and, if reinforced from now on, will be the basis for good sleep habits. Your baby will most likely be waking for one night feed. If it is not feed time, give your baby the chance to self soothe by not responding instantly to any small noise or squeak you may hear from her (leave her be for five minutes). If you allow her the opportunity to settle at these times, she will soon learn to self-calm and fall asleep again independently during the night.

FLEXIBLE ROUTINE FOR SIX TO TWELVE WEEKS

- Your baby will be feeding three- to four-hourly during the day.
- One of the night feeds (usually the 10-11 pm feed) will fall away and your baby will now sleep for a six- to seven-hour stretch before waking for a feed between 1 and 2 am.
- Provided she is gaining weight, do not give your baby milk if she cries or fusses

less than three hours after the last feed. Stretch the interval as close to four hours as you can by offering her 30-50 ml cooled, boiled water from a spoon or bottle, by encouraging hand-to-mouth or dummy sucking (non-nutritive), and by gently rocking and soothing her. Swaddle her in a cotton blanket or place her in a baby sling or pouch to keep her close to you.
- Expect a growth spurt at about six to eight weeks when you will have to feed more frequently over a period of approximately 24-48 hours.
- Limit her awake time to 60 to 80 minutes between day sleeps and plan your care giving, outings and stimulation around her sleeps.
- She should still be sleeping for 16 to 18 hours in a 24-hour cycle.

WHAT'S BABY UP TO?

Your baby's movements become more voluntary and are not ruled by reflexes to the same extent as before. At the beginning of this stage, your baby's movements feel and look very disorganized. She does not yet have control over her movements and has lost the feeling of security the curled-up foetal position gave her as a newborn. Towards the twelve-week mark her movements become more organized, as the ability to control her arms to swipe at objects starts developing. Swiping is important for eye-hand co-ordination and also helps develop the muscles of the arms. Your baby may even start reaching for objects within easy reach. Encourage her attempts, even though she is rarely successful at grasping anything.

SENSE-ABLE SECRET
Do not confuse hand or finger sucking with teething or hunger at this stage. Your baby will suck on her hands or fingers to self soothe and will explore her hands with interest.

Head control

The two-month-old works very hard to develop her head control. When lying on her back, she can hold her head in the midline to look at a mobile above her head. By lifting her head while on her tummy, your baby has sufficient opportunity to develop her back muscles. By three months she will be able to hold her head up at 45 degrees for a while when placed on her tummy. She will also hold her head up when sitting on your lap. Now is the time she starts to work hard on developing the strength of her tummy muscles. Achieving a balance between the back and stomach muscles is essential for rolling, a skill she will achieve at four to six months.

Visual development

Your baby can follow an object moving in an arc 15 cm from her face. She begins to follow you around the room with her eyes. During this period your baby will suddenly notice her hands. You will find her gazing at them and moving her fingers while watching the results.

This is the first active step in eye-hand co-ordination. She begins to explore her hands by putting them in her mouth. By three months your baby will recognize a bottle or the position and movements you make before breast-feeding. She will make eager, welcoming movements as she prepares to feed. She also now really enjoys bath time.

Socializing

At last the smiling, social baby you hoped for is here. She responds to your voice and makes throaty gurgles. By twelve weeks she will start to coo, squeal and even babble. She recognizes Mom and Dad and responds to your attention. She starts linking sounds with the object that makes them and will look to see where they are coming from.

ENHANCING DEVELOPMENT

Strengthening back and neck muscles is vital to promote head control now and crawling later on, so ensure that your baby spends time on her tummy now. If she doesn't spend time on her tummy in the early days, she will not be comfortable in this position later when she should be developing the muscles necessary for crawling. Another important skill developed at this stage is voluntary reaching. Encourage your baby to reach for and grasp objects by placing her under a baby gym or by placing interesting objects within reach.

As your baby gets older, she will have longer periods in the Calm-Alert state. A particular time of day will emerge when she is in the Calm-Alert state for a long stretch – often mid-morning (after her first sleep). Use this time to play with her and stimulate her a little with a new toy, or to go on a short outing.

If you are feeling a little cooped up, joining a massage class with your baby is a nice idea to get out, socialise and learn a new skill that will really enhance your baby's development.

A sensory diet

At this stage your baby is still very dependent on you to control the amount of stimulation she gets. While taking care that she does not become over-stimulated, you can start introducing some appropriate stimulation into her daily routine.

Encourage self-calming strategies that are starting to emerge. So if your baby is showing signs of self-calming by sucking her hands, don't intervene by popping her dummy in her mouth. Rather let her explore sucking to self-calm independently.

SENSE-ABLE SECRET
If your baby self-calms effectively from early on you may find that you do not need to offer her a dummy. But if she is slow to self-calm or is a fussy baby, a dummy provides the non-nutritive sucking that is important for calming. By giving your baby a dummy, you take some responsibility for calming her until she can put the dummy in her mouth independently. So she may go through a stage in the first year when she needs you to give her a dummy at night to go back to sleep.

ENVIRONMENT

Although your baby is more alert and ready for interaction, she is still sensitive to sensory input. Watch for signs of over-stimulation and protect her from overload by taking steps to provide a calmer environment.

SIGHT	• Geometric patterns, bright contrasting colours and faces are still what your baby will love to watch most. • Create a space where she can have 'visual down-time' with calming colours and no visual stimulation.
HEARING	• Your baby loves the sound of human voices, so speak to her a lot, using varied tones and interesting facial expressions. • Copy her noises and coos so that she knows that language is a two-way thing – this is the start of speech.
TOUCH	• Deep-touch pressure and touch on the back are calming. Tickle and light touch are stimulating, but watch for your baby's reaction – some children are sensitive to light and unpredictable touch and really don't enjoy it.
MOVEMENT	• Slow rhythmical movements are calming – use them before sleep times. Quick, irregular movements are alerting and should only be used during play. Only use these movements if your baby shows that she enjoys them.
MOTOR DEVELOPMENT	• To develop the back and tummy muscles, your baby needs to spend plenty of time on her tummy on the floor.

CAUTION

Make sure that objects you hang near your baby are safe – non-toxic and with no small pieces that can come off in her mouth.

ROUTINE-RELATED ACTIVITIES (TIMING)

Make both stimulating activities and calming strategies part of your daily caregiving programme.

SLEEP TIME

A quiet, calm sleep environment is essential for your baby to develop good sleep patterns, including both falling asleep with ease and staying asleep.

SIGHT	• Keep the visual world very calming around sleep time by dimming the lights, drawing the curtains and not putting visually stimulating toys in the cot.

HEARING	• The soothing sound of lullabies will calm her. • White noise CDs or household machines are a great idea to enhance sleep.
TOUCH	• Continue to swaddle your baby at night.
MOTOR DEVELOPMENT	• Alternate the side your baby sleeps on.

SLEEPING POSITION

Past generations of babies generally slept on their stomachs – a position that encourages the development of the back muscles from a young age. But research has shown that babies should not sleep face down on their tummies to minimize the risk of SIDS or cot death.

Lying flat on her back is a very inactive position, offering your baby no opportunity to develop her back muscles at all. In the side-lying position there will be more opportunity to develop the muscles that are important for rolling and crawling. Use foam wedges or a rolled-up towel to keep her in the side-lying position.

If there is a time of day when you will be very close to your baby and can check on her, for instance when you are reading or working next to her during a day sleep, let her sleep on her tummy.

NAPPY CHANGE TIME

This is a good time for visual stimulation, as your baby is lying awake and is ready to look around.

SIGHT	• Keep a black-and-white or brightly coloured mobile hanging above the changing mat. For variety, hang a changeable mobile above the mat, using a coat hanger with interesting objects securely tied to it.
HEARING	• Talk to your baby while changing her nappy.
MOTOR DEVELOPMENT	• Encourage her tummy muscles to work when you pick her up from the changing mat. Gently pull her into a sitting position with your hands on her shoulders so that she must hold her head up and even help a bit with her tummy muscles. (See illustration on the left.)

Bath time

Don't over-excite your baby at bath time since this is the start of the bedtime routine. Encourage Dad to participate in bath time as long as he does not over-stimulate her. Play quietly in the bath and then keep things very calm.

SIGHT	• You are your baby's favourite bath companion. Make eye-contact with her and show her bright, squeaky bath toys.
HEARING	• Recite nursery rhymes and sing to her while she's enjoying her bath.
TOUCH	• Massage your baby's limbs and stretch them out when you soap her before putting her in the bath. • Once in the bath, lightly massage her tummy and fill a sponge with water, squeezing it out over her body.
MOTOR DEVELOPMENT	• Encourage kicking and reaching for toys or your face while she is in the bath.

Awake time

As she spends more time awake, play quietly with her, especially when she is in the Calm-Alert state. You can stimulate her more and encourage longer periods of interaction, but do watch for signs that she's had enough.

SIGHT	• Use your facial expressions to teach your baby about her face. Encourage her to mimic your expressions. This copying and planning of a skilled movement is the start of motor planning. • Show her pictures of faces or geometric designs in black and red on white paper plates to help her focus. • Show your baby her hands – the first body parts she will realize belong to her – and play with her fingers so that she becomes aware of them. • Show her nature's mobiles: trees blowing in the wind and flowers nodding their bright heads. Also set up a mobile in the living room. • Prop her up on cushions for a while every day to give her another view of the world.
HEARING	• Recite nursery rhymes with an element of surprise: a few rhythmic, rhyming lines followed by an exclamation. Babies of this age love the feeling of anticipation followed by the surprise.

TOUCH	• Massage your baby when she is in the Calm-Alert state. Try to massage her at least twice a week, although a daily massage is ideal.
MOVEMENT	• Gently swing your baby round and up and down. Go at her pace and if she's not enjoying it, wait a few days before trying again.
MOTOR DEVELOPMENT	• Place your baby on her tummy each day with a mirror or an interesting toy to look at and reach for. If she is not keen at first, lie her on your tummy while you lie back at an angle. Each day lie further back until she's horizontal and really exercising her neck muscles. • To strengthen her tummy muscles, let her lie on her back and suspend a ball with bells near her feet. She'll be rewarded with movement and sound each time she kicks it, encouraging to her to try again. • Place rattles and toys with various textures in your baby's hands to help her develop an active grasp.

TRAVELLING TIME

As your baby approaches the three-month mark, you can explore more environments as you'll find that she is better at regulating stimuli.

SIGHT	• When out and about, let her see a bit of the world, only covering the front of the pram or baby chair with a nappy or blanket if she fusses or needs to sleep. • Put a mobile or baby mirror in her pram where she can see it and will be encouraged to reach for it. • Draw a bold face or design on a paper plate for her to focus on while in her baby seat in the car and attach it where she can see it.
HEARING	• Play a CD or tape of children's singing voices. Classical music (for example Majors for Minors) will be calming, especially on long car trips.
MOVEMENT	• When appropriate, carry your baby facing outwards in a pouch. She will enjoy the rhythm of your walking and the position encourages her to socialize and look around.
MOTOR DEVELOPMENT	• Always take her out of her baby seat when you reach your destination so that she does not remain in a static position.

SMELL	• If car trips distress your baby, use calming inputs such as placing a cotton wool swab dabbed with lavender or camomile oil in the car.

FEED TIME

If your baby becomes distracted during feeds, keep stimulation to a minimum.

SIGHT	• Pin a red or white ribbon to your clothes for her to focus on and fiddle with while she feeds.
HEARING	• If she becomes distracted and does not feed well, don't talk or have the television on during feeds. If she feeds well regardless of what is going on around her, do talk to or read to her so that she becomes familiar with language and tone changes in voice.
MOTOR DEVELOPMENT	• Alternate the side you feed on, even if you're bottle-feeding, to help develop both sides of her body equally.

TOYS AND TOOLS

You remain your baby's best toy and interaction provides the most fun and developmental input. Nevertheless, there are suitable toys you can make or buy.

SIGHT & HEARING	• Play gyms or mobiles with changeable or detachable objects. Make the objects on the mobile as interesting and colourful as possible with bright and contrasting colours to encourage your baby to look and to start reaching out. Include objects that make a noise to encourage her to reach for them. Securely attach a variety of objects to an upside-down umbrella or hanger, for example a tinfoil spiral cut from a tinfoil pie dish, a soft toy hanging face down on a string, an empty film container (with a tight lid) filled with rice grains, a mirror, colourful rattles, Christmas decorations, rubber washing-up glove with a face or black design drawn on it, a string of shells and other objects from nature, bird cage toys with bells, fabric balls and blocks. Avoid small objects which could choke your baby if detached.
TOUCH	• Textured toys provide tactile interest. Fill a sock with various items such as scrunched up plastic bags or beans and sew the opening securely closed. • Continue to put your baby on a texture mat (see page 103).

MOTOR DEVELOPMENT	• Include toys on the mobile that your baby will be encouraged to reach for. • Use your texture mat to make her tummy time on the floor interesting while she develops the muscles she needs for rolling.

COLIC REMEDIES

If your baby cries and you suspect that it is colic, first rule out basic causes of crying such as illness or hunger. In all likelihood your baby is tired or is suffering from over-stimulation. In this case follow these steps:

• Calm your baby's sensory environment by implementing a sensory diet.
• Establish a good daytime sleep routine to eliminate over-tiredness.
• Swaddle your baby and settle her to sleep.
• Help her access self-soothing strategies such as sucking on her fingers.
• Don't fuss with her too much by passing her from one person to another and burping her more than five minutes.
• If she is still crying after a long period of time, put her in a sling or pouch and pace with her until she falls asleep.

BABY'S FINE – HOW ARE YOU?

See page 103 if you think you may be suffering from perinatal distress.

Three to six months

Your baby's face lights up when he sees or hears you, and at last you feel that parenting is getting easier. Hopefully at this stage you are no longer getting up so often during the night and your baby's days are settling into a definite pattern with regular times for feeding, sleeping and playing.

You may now be faced with the reality of returning to the workplace. If you are returning to work you will need to choose a childcare option that suits your and your baby's needs.

To make the transition smoother, we suggest the following:
- Spend time introducing her to your baby's unique language so that she will understand his signals and act appropriately
- Draw up a routine for the caregiver to follow, based on your baby's age
- Explain the principles of sensory calming before sleep times, especially in the late afternoon
- Show her ideas for appropriate games and activities for awake time.

FEEDING

Although some mothers breast-feed for up to a year, others may decide introduce bottle-feeds at this time. If you are returning to work you may choose to express your breast milk or to introduce formula.

If you plan to do this, see page 44 for a simple formula to calculate how much milk to give your baby. By the end of this period, at the latest, **all** babies will need some form of solid food.

Expressing milk

Most mothers who return to the workplace are employed outside the home. If you are lucky enough to work from home, breast-feeding can continue with no interruptions. But if you cannot be with your baby while you are working, by expressing breast milk and leaving a supply for your baby, you can continue to give him the benefits of breast milk.

Even if you don't return to the workplace, expressing breast milk is an option should you occasionally want to take some time out, to attend a function without your baby, or simply have your hair done.

You will find details on expressing breast milk in Appendix B (see page 153) as well as in most general baby-care books (see also References and Recommended reading, page 157).

Introducing solids

There is no set time for introducing solids to your baby, however:
- Do not introduce solids if he is younger than four months; and

- Do not leave him on milk alone if he is older than six months; and
- Do not delay the introduction of solids to protect him against allergies – the latest research indicates that there is little evidence that this is effective.

Wait for your baby to show signs of hunger before introducing solids. The mere fact that he is four or five months old is no reason to start, provided he is a calm, contented baby, steadily gaining weight, feeding well during the day (four-hourly), and sleeping for eight to ten hours at a stretch at night without needing a feed.

If your baby suddenly needs more frequent feeding during both day and night, is older than four months and weighs in the region of 7 kg or more, these may be indications that he is looking for some extra 'fuel'. In that case, follow this easy five-step plan:

STEP 1

Begin with a single-grain baby cereal (rice or maize) as an evening meal. Mix a heaped teaspoon of the dry cereal with expressed breast milk, formula or cooled, boiled water to make a sloppy mixture. Once mixed, it will make about three teaspoonfuls. Offer it to your baby between 4 and 5 pm. Gradually increase the amount you give him each day, and adjust the consistency to suit his taste. If he is younger than five months, this may be all he needs at this stage to supply him with extra fuel. If he is older than five months, continue for two weeks and move on to Step 2.

STEP 2

At about 8 am, offer him the same amount of cereal that he is having in the evening. Continue with cereal in the morning and evening for the next two weeks. If he is younger than five months, wait for him to show you that he is hungry before adding this step – when he doesn't manage to stretch from his early morning feed until the next one in four hours' time.

STEP 3

Substitute the evening cereal with vegetables. Stick to vegetables with yellow or orange flesh (carrots, pumpkin, baby marrow, butternut, sweet potato), boiled or steamed and puréed with no extra salt or sugar and moistened with a little breast or formula milk if necessary. If your baby is younger than five months, give him cereal in the morning and vegetables in the evening until he shows signs of needing a third meal (see Step 4). If he is older than five months, continue with Step 3 for a week and move on to Step 4.

STEP 4

If he becomes hungry at lunchtime and cannot stretch from the mid-morning feed to the mid-afternoon feed but demands more milk at about 12 noon, offer him puréed fresh, raw fruit (banana, pear, papaya, avocado pear, mango, melon or steamed apples) at noon. Do not add extra sugar, but if necessary moisten with breast or formula milk. Offer the same amount as for breakfast and dinner solids. By now he is having three 'solid meals' a day, but his milk feeds remain the same (four-hourly). Continue with this meal plan for a further two weeks.

STEP 5

Introduce one tablespoon of natural yoghurt into any one meal of the day. Either mix it into his cereal, or add it to fresh fruit, or give it separately after vegetables. Continue with this diet until your baby is six months old. Do not give him proteins such as meat, chicken, cheese, eggs or fish. At this stage, solid food must in no way take the place of milk feeds. Solids are given in addition to breast or formula milk.

- Offer your baby solids when he is in a good mood, not when he is screaming for milk or is dog-tired.
- Respect his moods and feelings. Just as we have days when we don't feel very hungry, so do babies.
- Try not to let meal times become an issue between you and your baby.
- Don't force-feed. This will usually result in vomiting shortly thereafter.
- Introduce a single food at a time, about three times in a row, before introducing the next one.
- Generally, time the feed to be about one to two hours after a milk feed (which is also one to two hours before a milk feed).
- If your baby is sleeping, don't wake him up for a meal – rather delay it by an hour or skip it altogether.
- Invest in a hand-held blender. It will be very useful for a long time to come.

Weaning: from breast to bottle

For the purposes of this book we will regard weaning purely as moving from breast-feeding to bottle-feeding. The route you take can be either slow weaning which takes about two to four weeks, or 'Cold Turkey', replacing all breast-feeds with formula feeds within 24 hours.

You will find details in Appendix B (see page 153), as well as in most general baby-care books. Bear in mind that weaning may cause your baby to be unsettled and be prepared to spend more time calming him if necessary.

SLEEP

As long as your baby is not ill and he is thriving, he will be able to sleep for six to eight hours at night before needing another feed. Try to stretch this period by patting him back to sleep, and encourage non-nutritive sucking on his hand or a dummy.

If your baby wakes more often, exclude any other causes of night waking by going through the process of elimination (see page 56) before simply offering him a feed.

He will have three or four sleeps during the day, determined by his awake time of about 90 minutes. If he still needs help to go to sleep, now is the time to teach him some self-calming measures, and ensure he goes to sleep for both his day and night sleeps happily awake.

FLEXIBLE ROUTINE FOR THREE TO SIX MONTHS

- Your baby will be feeding three- to four-hourly during the day.
- Provided he is not ill and is gaining weight, don't feed your baby if he is crying or fussing less than four hours since the last feed. Stretch the period to as close to four hours as you can by offering him 50 to 80 ml of cooled, boiled water from a spoon or bottle, encouraging non-nutritive sucking (hand-to-mouth or dummy) and by gently rocking and soothing him. Swaddle him in a cotton blanket, or place him in a baby carrier to keep him close to you.
- The second night feed (1 to 2 am) may fall away.
- Expect a growth spurt at about four months, when you will need to feed him more frequently for 24 to 48 hours.
- If he remains hungry, consider introducing a supplementary feed, changing his formula or introducing solids.
- Limit his awake time to between 80 and 90 minutes and plan your care-giving, outings and stimulation within this time.
- He should sleep for four to five hours during the day, divided into three to four sleeps, and for 10 to 12 hours at night (a total of 15 to 16 hours in a 24-hour cycle).

MEAL PLAN	
	If you have started your baby on solids and he has graduated to three meals a day (this may take anything from two weeks to three months) his basic meal plan may look like this:
6 am	Breast/bottle
8 am	Breakfast: cereal/yoghurt
10 am	Breast/bottle (if he appears to want to drop this feed, give him less breakfast)
12 noon	Lunch: fruit/yoghurt
2 pm	Breast/bottle (if he appears to want to drop this feed, give him less lunch)
4 pm	Dinner: vegetables/yoghurt
6 pm	Breast/bottle
7 pm	Bedtime. He should easily sleep for eight to 10 hours without needing more milk feeds.

WHAT'S BABY UP TO?

As the primitive reflexes disappear altogether, your baby starts to use and direct his body to learn about his world. He can hold his head in the midline when lying on his back and starts to bring his hands to the middle. This is the beginning of co-ordinating the two sides of his body – an early foundation for skipping!

Your baby is now very visually alert – he is interested in anything new. Suddenly he will be very distractible during feed times and milk feeds may have to be given in the peace and quiet of a bedroom or at least with no interesting people or conversations around him. He will recognize people and thrive on familiarity. He understands and enjoys routine. His concentration span is increasing too, and he spends more time examining and playing with an object.

Muscles and movement

When he is on his tummy he will push up on his elbows and may even start to push up on straight arms. He may also start to reach for objects in this position and then collapse over his supporting arm, which causes him to roll over onto his back accidentally. In the same way, when lying on his back he will have such fun grasping his toes and, whilst checking out those wiggly things at the end of his feet, may lose his balance, rolling over half-way to the side. This accidental rolling is the start of a very important milestone, rolling, which will start to emerge during this stage. By six months your baby should be rolling one way (usually tummy to back) and maybe even both ways.

Playing with his feet is important for other reasons too. This is how he develops his tummy muscles. Similarly, when lying and playing on his tummy, he lifts his head and thereby develops his back muscles. This is vital for rolling and crawling, which are amongst the most important milestones of the first year.

Up to three months of age your baby probably did not bear any weight on his legs, but now he will love to stand supported on your lap. Towards six months he'll love to bounce in this position. This is his way of exercising the muscles needed for pulling himself up to stand. All movement stimulation now becomes fun and your baby will love movement games. It is important that you stimulate this sense because the vestibular system is important for the development of muscle tone and movement co-ordination.

Sitting and manipulating

Your baby will learn to sit at around this time, making your life much easier. At first he'll need support and will often lean forward on his hands for support while sitting up. By six months he will sit unsupported. At around the same time, he will begin reaching intentionally and his hands will become useful tools. He will be able to manipulate toys – holding and turning them. He will hold objects in his whole hand (palmer grasp) and will start to bang them. Soon he will start to use his thumb and index finger to pinch and poke objects. He cannot yet let go of objects voluntarily.

Mouths are fun

His grasp of objects is crude but he can get all manner of things to his mouth! Don't mistake this as a sign of hunger or early teething. He simply uses his gums and lips to explore objects and learn about their shape and texture. The touch receptors in the mouth are more finely tuned than anywhere else on the body at this stage, and he learns about his world through his mouth.

He'll also discover what fun his mouth is, realizing it's not just good for exploring, but also as a playmate. He'll play with his saliva, blow bubbles and play with sounds. He'll discover that he can imitate some of your sounds too and will start to make vowel sounds. This is the start of babbling. This is the stage when your baby really loves to laugh and will squeal and chuckle with delight.

ENHANCING DEVELOPMENT

At this stage working on his sitting, balance and rolling skills is a priority. Rolling is vital for all other development. Other important tasks to develop are voluntary grasp and eventually voluntary release. The hands need objects of different shapes, sizes, weights and textures to develop a wide variety of grasps. For instance, the type of grasp needed for a large, soft block is very different from that for a small pea. Be sure to encourage both big and small grasps.

Use plenty of visual and auditory input. The eye muscles are more developed, so your baby can focus quite well. Encourage the development of eye movements by providing opportunities for tracking a moving object. Your baby will also start to fine-tune his auditory skills, listening to sounds and attaching meaning to them. As he approaches six months, he'll love to be rocked, rolled over, swung and generally moved about. All this movement input is vital for his muscle development and also his spatial perception. Encourage a lot of movement from now on, as this is vital for the development of gross motor skills later.

A sensory diet

Your baby now spends much more time awake and in the Calm-Alert state. Use some of that time to encourage development by providing structured stimulation. At this stage your baby moves from the very introspective and somewhat visual stage to a more alert phase where he seeks sensory input.

ENVIRONMENT

From three months your baby is able to cope with more stimulation from his environment. If he has suffered from colic, it will more than likely abate now.

SIGHT	• Start introducing your baby to visually more interesting places and objects, but watch for signs of over-stimulation.
HEARING	• Talk to him about what you are doing or what you see in as much detail as possible, using an exaggerated tone. • Use his name over and over so that he learns it – soon he'll love the sound of his name. • Share jokes and laughter with your baby, as this is the stage that humour starts to develop.
TOUCH	• Don't stop him from mouthing objects as this is an important learning process. • Keep a small basket or container in each room filled with different objects with different textures and sounds.
MOTOR DEVELOPMENT	• Time on the floor continues to be vital for motor development to achieve milestones such as sitting, rolling and moving between these positions.

ROUTINE-RELATED ACTIVITIES (TIMING)

Make both stimulating activities and calming strategies part of your daily care-giving programme. The emphasis may slowly shift from calming to stimulating

SLEEP TIME

Your baby can now cope with more stimulation during the day but he may still need help to calm down to a relaxed, Drowsy state for sleep.

SIGHT	• Keep the room visually calming around bedtime and avoid visual stimulation just before sleeps (day and night).
HEARING	• Sing quiet lullabies and play soft, soothing music which he will enjoy while falling asleep.
TOUCH	• Ensure that blankets, bedding and sleepwear are soft and have no scratchy seams. A rough seam on a vest may be all it takes to wake your baby between sleep cycles. Cover the bottom sheet with a soft receiving blanket.
SMELL	• The calming scent of camomile and lavender can be used in your baby's room to enhance sleep. Use a burner with essential oils or a scented room spray.

MOVEMENT	• Continue to use slow, rhythmic movements before sleep times and to calm your baby. Put him down when he is drowsy, but awake.

NAPPY CHANGE TIME

Your baby will really enjoy looking at objects and touching them when lying on his back for a nappy change.

SIGHT	• Keep the changeable mobile hanging over the changing mat. When your baby is nearing five months, encourage his hands to move to midline and reach out by attaching interesting objects to the mobile with elastic so that he can reach out, grasp and pull the object towards himself.
HEARING	• Describe what you are doing at the changing mat, for example "I am putting on your top, now your pants..."
MOTOR development	• To encourage rolling, use components of the movement while dressing him. Bend his leg slightly and roll him onto his side, place the nappy under him and roll him back. • For neck control and tummy strength, hold his arms and gently pull him into a sitting position.

BATH TIME

Bath time remains the start of the bedtime routine, so don't over-excite your baby. Rather play quietly and then be very calm after the bath.

TOUCH	• While your baby is naked or just wearing a nappy, touch various parts of his body with different textures, for example brushes, various fabrics, gloves, sponges. • Choose textured bath toys, such as different sponges, loofahs and plastic toys. Pet toys often have an interesting texture – for example a fish with spikes. • After bath, rub him down well for all-over touch input and give him a baby massage.
MOVEMENT	• The tactile sensation and warmth of the bath water create a containing environment ideal for introducing movement. Sway him backwards and forwards in the bath.
SMELL	• Use baby bath products with a calming scent such as lavender and camomile.

Awake time

As your baby gets older he will enjoy longer stretches of Calm-Alert time and you can start to stimulate him a little more now. But tune in to his signals and give him quiet space if necessary.

SIGHT	• Play games to encourage visual tracking, such as bobbing a ball across his field of vision, rolling a ball past or away from him, shining a torch on the wall, or blowing bubbles. Also point out interesting objects around the house or garden, or cars or animals in motion. • Play peek-a-boo games – briefly covering a toy or his face, then uncovering it (use textured fabric for variation).
HEARING	• Use bells, rattles and your voice, moving the source of the sound, to help him fine-tune his listening skills. • Recite rhymes and sing songs with an element of surprise. (See Appendix C, page 155 for nursery rhymes.)
TOUCH	• Let your baby play and roll on different surfaces, for instance grass, a lambskin mat, and coir.
MOVEMENT	• Carry him in various positions, rock him, dance around the room with him and play aeroplanes by manoeuvring him around in the air (slowly at first). • Play plenty of bouncing games with your baby standing or sitting on your lap. Combine this with action rhymes ('This is the way the lady rides'). • Gently rock him over a large ball, or roll him in a blanket and unroll him. Pull him around in a box and swing him in a hammock.
MOTOR DEVELOPMENT	• When he's sitting supported, encourage him to reach for toys placed just beyond his reach. Help him to practise sitting by propping him up with pillows, removing some as his balance improves. • Let him play on the floor often to encourage muscle development and place him on his tummy to strengthen his back and neck muscles in preparation for crawling. Put a mobile, rattle, baby mirror or ball in front of him. If he dislikes this position, place a rolled-up towel under his chest at first or sit on the floor and lay him over your leg in a crawling position and rock him to and fro.

SENSE-ABLE SECRET
Babies who are used to being on their tummies crawl sooner, as their back and neck muscles are stronger.

MOTOR development	• Play another version of aeroplanes: lie on your back with your knees pulled towards your chest and place him tummy down on your shins, holding his arms. • Play give-and-take games to improve his holding and release of objects.

CAUTION	If the movements are too rough or your baby is very sensitive to movement stimuli, he will cry or look anxious because he is being disorganized by the input. Don't let him avoid movement altogether, but always play within his pleasure zone.

TRAVELLING TIME

Your baby is now ready for more interaction with the outside world. He will enjoy trips out and visits to new places, but his tolerance for new and exciting experiences is still quite limited.

SIGHT	• When your baby is awake, don't cover the baby seat or pram. Let him follow moving objects to help develop his eye muscles. • If you are out at sleep time, cover the pram as before or turn him to face you in the pouch or baby sling.
HEARING	• Play a CD or tape of children's singing voices or classical music in the car.
TOUCH	• Attach a texture mobile to the grab-handle above the car window. Use a hanger with interestingly textured toys tied to it with string so that your baby can play with them while sitting in his car seat.
MOTOR development	• When you carry or hold your baby, offer less support by holding him lower down on his body so that his stomach and neck muscles must work to keep him upright. • Don't leave him in a baby seat for long periods, as this position is too passive and does not encourage tummy and back muscles to work.

FEED TIME

Your baby may become quite distracted during milk feeds. Restrict sensory input to ensure efficient feeding. He starts exploring new textures with his mouth as solids become part of his diet.

Sight	• If visual input distracts him, feed him in a dull, non-stimulating environment for a while.
Touch	• Once he starts wearing a bib he will feel it with his hands and mouth, so choose bibs with an interesting texture. • Feeling solids in his mouth may make him gag initially, so start with runny cereal. He will have to move on to more lumpy food later, so try to purée vegetables and fruit yourself as the texture is not as smooth as that of commercially available bottled baby food.
Motor development	• Encourage his ability to grip small items by giving him a variety of finger foods such as carrots and slices of apple. He probably won't eat them but will enjoy gnawing away at them. Watch him closely in case he chokes.

TOYS AND TOOLS

Research has shown that playing with a wide variety of toys with different textures and functions enhances development. This does not mean that you must rush out and spend a fortune on toys. What it means is that you must offer your baby a wide variety of experiences – especially in terms of touch.

Sight	• Let your baby look at books with simple, brightly coloured pictures. Hard board and waterproof books are practical as your baby is likely to want to mouth them. Pictures of faces in books and magazines will fascinate him. Let him look at his own face in mirrors. • Use puppets to develop visual and language skills. • Baby gyms or mobiles with dangling toys encourage focus, reach and grasp.
Hearing	• Read to him from books and let him listen to songs to encourage language development. • CDs of music enhance many areas of brain development • Give him rattles to hold and manipulate to make a noise.
Touch	• Use play mats with different textures, for instance a lambskin rug. • Make a 'sensory snake' by filling a long sock with items that feel and sound different: a scrunched-up plastic bag, pasta shapes, cotton wool and so on. Sew it closed and sew patches of different textured fabrics on the outside. Ensure that he can't get any of the contents out as he may choke.

MOVEMENT	• Buy a large ball for him to play on and roll over. • Put up a swing in the garden or in the house. Suspend two meters of lycra fabric as a hammock. Your baby will love its soothing feel and rocking motion. • Play baby go-carting by sitting your baby in an open box lined with cushions and pulling the box behind you.
MOTOR DEVELOPMENT	• Place him on his tummy on his textured floor mat. • Make a mobile with toys tied to it with elastic so that your baby can pull them towards himself.

<table>
<tr><td>IMPORTANCE OF CRAWLING</td><td>

During the next four months your baby should start to crawl. To ensure that your baby is well prepared for crawling, give him lots of tummy time to strengthen his muscles. He should crawl for as long as possible, as crawling lays the foundation for many other skills.

• By taking weight on his hands, your baby develops stability in his shoulders and develops the arches of his hands. This is important for fine motor skills like holding a pencil and drawing later.

• Crawling provides a wealth of touch input through his hands and at times through his entire body. Babies who dislike touch or are tactile defensive sometimes avoid crawling for this reason.

• By being mobile from a young age, your baby starts to plan how to get to things and how to achieve certain positions. This is important for motor planning which is essential for learning new skills later on, such as riding a bike or learning to skip.

• By crawling low on the ground your baby can get into awkward places, which teaches him about his body size and therefore develops spatial awareness. Spatial awareness is in turn important for learning to read, write and do maths later.

• Crawling requires the co-ordinated use of the two sides of the body. It therefore promotes the development of the left and right brain and the connections between them. This is vital for co-ordination later, such as that involved in skipping.

</td></tr>
</table>

BABY'S FINE – HOW ARE YOU?

See page 103 if you think you may be suffering from perinatal distress.

Six to nine months

This stage of your baby's life is one of the most rewarding. She openly communicates with you, with plenty of smiles, giggles and laughs. She's starting to reach out to grasp toys and her little body is becoming strong enough to enable her to sit and play contentedly, or to lie on her back and suck her toes quite happily. Enjoy this very special time – it's the calm before the storm. The next stage, when she becomes mobile, adds a new dimension to the word 'hectic'!

FEEDING

The exciting world of solid food now really opens up before your little gourmet. New ingredients, tastes and textures add variety and necessary nutrition.

If you haven't yet started your baby on solid food, you shouldn't wait any longer. Although breast or formula milk still plays an important role and must not be excluded from her diet, now that she is six months old, milk alone is no longer adequate nutrition. Follow the plan as laid out on page 115. Introduce the five steps over a period of two to three weeks, before moving on to the diet plan for six to nine months.

If your six-month-old has been on solids for some time already, it is time to make some changes.

More variety

The introduction of more textured food will encourage and develop your baby's chewing and mashing skills. This will help to develop muscle control of the tongue, lips and cheeks, which is a vital part of speech development.

This is also the time to introduce finger foods which encourage fine-motor control in little fingers and develop the taste receptors in your baby's mouth to manage more tasty and textured foods. Give finger foods at the end of a meal or as a small snack between meals.

If your baby has teeth, don't give her any finger foods that will break off into hard bits and not soften in her mouth. Try rice cakes, finger biscuits, toast, peeled soft fruit, celery, sun-dried fruit (mango strips) and biltong sticks. Give her apple, carrot and cucumber sticks only if she has no teeth.

All the food groups

To enhance your baby's growth and development, protein must be added to her diet at this stage. She will need eight to ten teaspoons of protein combined with a variety of carbohydrates, fats, fruit and vegetables, spread over three meals a day. Both animal proteins (dairy products, meat, poultry and fish) and vegetable proteins (legumes, dried beans and nuts – ground or in paste form) are suitable. She can have egg yolk from six months of age and whole egg a few weeks later.

Don't add any additional sugar or salt to your baby's food. Get into the habit of reading labels and avoid foods with sweeteners, colourants and preservatives. Avoid processed foods, packaged sauces and spices.

CAUTION

If you have a family history of allergies or your baby shows signs of allergies (see page 58), certain proteins such as legumes, some nuts, fish, soy and eggs are best avoided until your baby turns at least one year old. You should also seek expert advice with regard to a hypoallergenic diet.

Milk

If you are still breast-feeding your baby, there is no reason to stop unless you are ready to doing so. Your breast milk will adapt to her changing nutritional needs, and as her solid food diet improves, her demand for breast milk will decrease. The same applies to formula milk, but you do need to change to a formula specifically for babies aged six months and older. This milk contains more protein and will cater for her growing needs.

Your baby's minimum milk requirement (breast or formula) is approximately 500 ml per day. If she is not enthusiastic about breast-feeds or formula milk, there is ample opportunity to include milk in her three daily meals. She will most likely drop the mid-morning milk feed, so expect her to be on just three milk feeds at this stage.

IDEAS FOR MEALS

BREAKFAST

- Baby cereal or cooked oats, maize meal, Taystee Wheat, Maltabella or millet porridge plus two to three teaspoons of protein (cottage cheese, yoghurt, egg yolk, ground almonds, formula milk)
- Bread with egg
- Fresh fruit, yoghurt and ground almonds or puréed dates

LUNCH AND DINNER

- Avocado pear, fresh fruit and cottage or cream cheese
- Bread with egg
- Vegetable soup with bread
- Fresh fruit, yoghurt or custard with almonds, pumpkin or sesame seeds
- Mashed potato with cheese sauce, sprinkled with ground almonds or sesame seeds
- Macaroni cheese, mince or fish bake
- Corn rice or brown rice with creamed spinach or cheese sauce
- Casserole – lamb, chicken or bean
- Chicken broth and vegetables

Supplements

Babies are born with iron stores that run out by the time they reach four to six months of age. As there is no iron present in breast milk, it is important to give your baby an **iron supplement** when she reaches this age. Even babies on formula milk need iron supplementation, because the quantity of milk decreases as solids take preference. Infant cereals are iron-fortified, as are some varieties of fruit and vegetable juices.

Extra plant protein is also beneficial. Liquid supplements of plant protein such as Barley Green have been shown to improve growth and development.

Essential fatty acids are important to nourish your baby's growing brain and eyes and to help with the transmission of brain signals. It is a good idea to supplement her diet with an omega 3 and 6 supplement. Ask your pharmacist to recommend one that is suitable for babies.

The first teeth (lower central incisors, followed by the top central incisors) usually emerge between six and nine months. Your baby may develop a slightly runny nose and loose stools, with a red rash around the mouth and on the nappy area. Cool spare dummies and teethers in the fridge and let her chew on them to soothe inflamed gums. She doesn't need special teething medication unless she's running a temperature, in which case you should seek medical advice.

Clean her teeth gently with a small amount of baby toothpaste on your finger or a silicone finger brush (obtainable from baby shops). There's no need to rinse. In South Africa, all toothpaste has fluoride added, so there is no need to supplement her diet with fluoride unless your dentist recommends it.

To prevent decay, don't dip dummies or teethers in sweet substances, or let your baby fall asleep with a bottle or give her sweet snacks. Give her chewy food as chewing massages gums and promotes the flow of saliva to cleanse teeth.

SLEEP

This is often the stage when sleep becomes a problem, caused partly by separation anxiety, but also by disruptions in sleep habits owing to teething. Both of these can result in habit-forming night wakings. If your baby is waking up at night, address the problem before it becomes a big issue that is harder to manage.

Provided she is following the eating plan discussed, she will be able to sleep for 10-12 hours at night without needing a feed, so don't be tempted to feed her if she wakes. If she is still waking during the night, go through the process of elimination (see page 56) to exclude possible causes of distress, then teach her self-calming strategies.

If she is still struggling to fall asleep by herself at bedtime, go back to setting the stage for sleep. If this does not work, sleep coaching may be necessary (see pages 51-54). Never lose track of the importance of day sleeps and keeping to her appropriate awake times.

Expect some restless nights when she is teething.

Dummy patrol

If your baby uses a dummy as an effective means of self-soothing during the night, you may need to be on dummy patrol for a while. Until she is old enough to use her dummy independently at night, accept dummy patrol as a normal stage of parenting. She will be ready for you to help her to use her dummy independently at night from around the age of seven months.

- In the first few days, keep putting her dummy in her mouth when she cries at night, but during the day never put the dummy directly into her mouth. Rather place it in her hand so that she learns to put it in her mouth herself.
- Attach her dummy onto a dummy ribbon or dummy chain during waking hours, so that is available for her if she needs it. When she needs her dummy, guide her hand onto the ribbon or chain until she finds it herself. Be patient; with time, she will learn to pop it in herself in daylight hours.
- Once she has achieved this independence during daytime, do the same at night – never place it in her mouth, but rather put the dummy or dummy chain or ribbon in her hand so she must take the final step of putting the dummy in her mouth on her own.
- When she wakes for the first time expecting the dummy, wait for about a minute before responding to her. A dim night light in her room may help her to see her dummy when she wakes. Make sure that there are plenty of spare dummies placed in her cot, so that she can spot them easily on waking. If she does not succeed in finding her dummy herself, go to her and help her to find it independently.
- The next time she wakes expecting the dummy, wait slightly longer before responding to her, giving her a bit more time to find it independently. If she does not succeed, go and help her.
- With each subsequent waking, wait for a slightly longer period of time (add a minute or two) before responding to her. This time period allows her an opportunity to learn how to find her dummy independently.
- Be prepared for a few nights of disturbed sleep until you get this right – but persevere, it's worth it!

FLEXIBLE ROUTINE FOR SIX TO NINE MONTHS

- Your baby will be having three meals a day: breakfast, lunch and supper.
- Her milk feeds will drop to one on waking, one after lunch and one at bedtime.
- She will enjoy finger food snacks at mid-morning and mid-afternoon.
- She will sleep for 10 to 12 hours at night without requiring a feed. If she is

still waking at night, follow the sleep coaching recommendations on page 52 provided she is thriving and is not ill. Teething may cause restless nights.

- She will still need two to three naps during the day.
- Limit her awake time between sleeps during the day to approximately 2 hours, and plan your care-giving, outings and stimulation within this time.
- She should be sleeping for 14 to 16 hours in a 24-hour cycle.

Her meal plan may look like this (refer to *Ideas for meals* on page 128):

6 am	Breast/formula milk
8 am	Breakfast
10 am	Juice/water/camomile or rooibos tea and snack
12 noon	Lunch
2 pm	Breast or formula milk
3-4 pm	Juice/water/camomile or rooibos tea and snack
5 pm	Dinner
6-7 pm	Breast or formula milk

WHAT'S BABY UP TO?

When your six-month-old baby is placed on her back she works hard at developing her tummy muscles for sitting and crawling. She loves lifting her legs and holding on to her feet, and lifts her head to look at her feet. All the tummy and back muscle exercises will now pay off, as your baby rolls both from tummy to back, and back to tummy. Towards eight months she will start complaining when you put her on her back and nappy changing may become a real challenge as she tries to roll over on to her tummy. She can **sit** unsupported and by nine months she can get in and out of a sitting position on her own.

Movement and manipulation

While sitting, your baby starts reaching to get a toy and will even turn to the side and retrieve a toy a little distance away. This is how she'll one day find herself in the **crawling** position – she'll reach too far and end up on all fours. In this position, she may spend a bit of time rocking before collapsing on to her tummy. A few more days of rocking on all fours and she'll just set off, usually crawling backwards first. How your baby reaches the crawling position does not matter. She may belly-creep first, or go from tummy-lying into a crawling position. What is important is that she does crawl. By nine months she should be well into crawling mode.

Held in a standing position, she can support her weight fully and loves to bounce, move and sway. Any movement stimulation becomes a fun game for most babies and they love nursery rhymes which involve movement, such as 'This is the way the lady rides'. Other enjoyment is found in toys. Now that she

SENSE-ABLE SECRET
Don't limit your baby's explorations unless she is endangering herself or others. Exploring the environment is an important means of learning about the world.

can pass toys from hand to hand and **manipulate** objects, she loves to hold anything. In addition to exploring objects with her mouth, she examines them more purposefully with her hands.

Object permanence

Your baby sees detail well and recognizes things in her environment. As she approaches eight months of age, she starts to experience stranger anxiety and notices as soon as you are out of sight – she does not realize that you still exist when she can't see you. But by nine months, she will develop object permanence – the awareness that something still exists when it is out of sight. So now she'll look around for a dropped toy and will love peek-a-boo games.

Your social butterfly

Your baby is turning into a real chatterbox. A singsong babble, chuckles and irritated screams are all part of her new verbal repertoire. She may even begin to imitate conversations. She knows her name and understands what 'No' means. She also starts to understand social situations and waves goodbye.

She may now have a strong attachment to a security object such as a blanket or soft toy. This is a positive sign of her growing independence as she uses it for self-calming.

ENHANCING DEVELOPMENT

Your baby works hard at becoming more mobile. She is motivated to move around, begins to pivot on her tummy and creep and crawl. Bilateral hand use starts to develop at this stage. She is a social being but needs to grasp the idea that you still exist even when you leave the room. There is much emphasis on the acquisition of motor skills now and the focus will fall on the tasks of sitting well and crawling. This is often an easier period with your baby as she is more content in play. Implementing a routine is important at this stage, as your baby thrives when she has a familiar structure to her day. Encourage the achievement of vital milestones such as rolling and crawling, as they lay important foundations for future development.

A sensory diet

As your baby can handle more and more sensory input you can begin to stimulate her more. Always watch her closely for warning signals of over-stimulation and feelings of insecurity. This may be a harrowing time as sleep problems often arise during this stage.

ENVIRONMENT

As your baby gets older, her environment should become more stimulating than calming, except around sleep times.

SIGHT	• Place only one or two toys in front of her so that she can play constructively and does not become overwhelmed.
HEARING	• Keep talking to your baby even when you're out of sight so she can learn that you still exist when she can't see you.
MOTOR DEVELOPMENT	• Tie a string onto a toy so that she can pull it towards herself and retrieve it independently.

ROUTINE-RELATED ACTIVITIES (TIMING)

Include stimulating activities and calming strategies in your daily care-giving programme. Stimulating activities begin to feature more prominently.

SLEEP TIME

Even though your baby can cope with more sensory input and still remain in a Calm-Alert state, limit stimulation before bedtime, especially if she is a very alert child.

SIGHT	• The room should still be decorated in calming colours and darkened by block-out lining on the curtains or blinds, with no visually stimulating items in or too near the cot.
TOUCH	• Use soft blankets, bedding and clothing. • Use a sleeping bag from six months onwards so that your baby is kept at a constant temperature at night – babies of this age tend to kick their blankets off. • Find a soft toy or blanket as a security object to which she can become attached and use for self-calming at night. • If your baby has the odd really bad night's sleep and the process of elimination gives you no clue as to why, make a note of what she was wearing that night. Sometimes it's an irritating label or scratchy fabric that's responsible.

NAPPY CHANGE TIME

Towards the end of this stage your baby will start to resist being placed on her back for nappy changes.

SIGHT	• Fun mobiles with changeable pieces that are within reach are great for this age. Babies love looking at them, and being able to touch what they see is rewarding for them.
HEARING	• If you have a music mobile over the changing mat, wind it up for her to listen to when you change her nappy.

MOTOR DEVELOPMENT	• To teach your baby to sit up from lying down, after a nappy change hold one of her arms and roll her towards the other side and up into a sitting position. This teaches her muscles the feeling of the movement.

BATH TIME

Bath time remains the start of the bedtime routine, so be careful not to over-excite your baby at this time of day; rather play quietly and then be very calm after her bath.

SIGHT	• Place bath toys in the bath so that she can watch them floating towards her and away from her to develop her eye muscles for tracking.
HEARING	• Sing and talk to your baby. Start labelling her body parts as you wash them in the bath.
TOUCH	• Use touch to draw her attention to a body part – rub her tummy firmly with a facecloth or put bubbles on it and encourage her to reach for them. • Add the fun of a bubble-bath for a new texture to explore.
MOTOR DEVELOPMENT	• Use a commercially available bath support or non-slip mat to ensure she does not slip and fall under the water and never leave her alone whilst she's in the bath. • She will enjoy pouring which is excellent for developing muscles in the shoulder, so give her plastic beakers that are small enough to handle and tip.
SMELL	• Use lavender or camomile scented bath products for a calming effect before her bedtime.

AWAKE TIME

Use her awake time as playtime for varied stimulation. She is ready to deal with more sensory input and, if she is in the Calm-Alert state, will learn a lot about her world.

SIGHT	• As she now loves outings, take her out in her pram or pouch and point out and describe interesting things to her. • To encourage eye-tracking and strengthen her eye muscles, play games where she can watch a ball roll away or point out a moving aeroplane or car. • She will enjoy hiding games. To help her grasp the idea of object permanence, partially or completely hide objects for her to find.
HEARING	• Show your baby where sounds are coming from so that she attaches meaning to the sounds she hears. • When talking to your baby, use exaggerated tones and gestures and copy the sounds she makes. • Read books to her, showing her their bright pictures. • In the kitchen, while you're cooking, sit her on the floor with pots and pans to bang on. Give her other objects that make interesting noises. • Use puppets to encourage communication. • Give her soft toys that play music or squeak. • Recite rhymes that actively involve her. Try 'Pat-a-cake', 'Incy-wincy spider', and others that encourage the anticipation of actions.
TOUCH	• Turn a walk into a feely tour, letting her feel the various textures in the environment such as leaves, nests and so on. Use the feely tour to illustrate the qualities of things, for example soft leaf, rough sand, wet grass. • Sing finger and toe songs such as 'Round and round the garden' and 'This little piggy'. • Keep a variety of touch-stimulation objects for her to play with in each room of the house.
MOVEMENT	• Go on a swing with your baby and move it in all directions. • Put your baby onto an entertaining moving toy such as a fair-sized push-along truck; always support her as she sits on the back. • Help her to pull herself up to stand on your lap and let her bounce if she enjoys this. • Jolly-jumpers are controversial in that they encourage bad patterns of standing and bearing weight in some children. If in doubt, don't use them. If you put your baby in a jolly-jumper for some movement stimulation, do so for not more than 10 minutes each day, never leaving your baby to jump unsupervised.

MOTOR DEVELOPMENT	• Sit her on the grass or carpet and let her reach for toys around her. This promotes sitting balance and encourages her to crawl. • Now is the time to start swimming lessons if you wish to. The time spent with you in a warm pool is wonderfully stimulating for all the senses and her motor development. • To improve her sitting balance, sit her on your lap and slowly raise one of your legs fractionally, just enough to elicit a balance reaction without causing her to fall over. • Encourage her to crawl by placing toys just out of reach. Let her spend time on her tummy, or place her on all fours over your leg and rock her in this position, giving her a sense of the movement. Encourage her to crawl over obstacles such as pillows, blankets and you. • Develop hand function by giving her items with interesting shapes to handle. Play clapping rhymes ('Clap handies', 'Pat-a-cake'). • Encourage the use of both hands together by tearing paper, such as phone book pages. Put stickers on your baby's hands for her to pull off. Place an object in each of her hands, or give her one big object which she will only be able to hold using two hands.

TRAVELLING TIME

Use music and toys to make journeys interesting for your baby. She will love outings in the pram or baby carrier.

SIGHT	• As your baby may start to resist being put in the car seat, distract her visually with a mobile of natural objects that make interesting noises or feel interesting, such as seed pods and feathers. Hang this from the grab handle above the window.
HEARING	• Invest in a good quality CD of children's singing.
MOVEMENT	• If your baby gets car-sick or dislikes the motion of the car it could be that she is hypersensitive to vestibular input. Help her cope by using calming strategies like sucking (dummy, juice in a bottle or cup with a straw). Very cold liquids help for motion sickness. You can also place a cotton-wool swab with a few drops of lavender oil in the ashtray for a calming smell.

FEED TIME

Feed time is a great opportunity for exploration now. It's also a great advantage that the object she puts to her mouth actually tastes nice!

TOUCH	• Allow your baby to enjoy texture play with foodstuffs such as spaghetti, other soft pasta shapes, lumpy custard, jelly, watermelon, coloured ice, chocolate pudding and cereal. Describe the qualities of the food to her.
MOTOR DEVELOPMENT	• Handling finger food is one of the first things your baby can do for herself and she'll love it. Encourage fine motor control by giving her small pieces of food, but watch that she doesn't choke. • In the high chair your baby starts to practise release of toys by dropping them. You can attach a string to the toy and teach her how to pull it up again.

TOYS AND TOOLS

This is a very short list of some useful toys. There is such a vast toy market for this age group that we cannot mention all the wonderful items out there. You don't need a great number of toys at once. Let your baby become familiar with a few toys and then rotate them. She will 'forget' toys that have been put away and then 'rediscover' them. This is an especially good idea after holidays and birthdays when children get many gifts.

SIGHT	• Give her books with bright, clear pictures, preferably board books or plastic books that will survive chewing. • Make personalized books using photos of 'her things' (cup, mom, phone, bed). • Books with plastic cords that tie on to the pram are excellent for travel time as they won't get lost or dropped out of the pram. • To help her grasp object permanence, make or buy toys that disappear and reappear, such as a pop-up toy. Draw a face on a wooden spoon that you slip inside an empty toilet roll. Push the spoon up to make the face appear at the top of the roll, then pull it back so it disappears.
HEARING	• Rattles and bells. • CDs of songs and music. • Pictures of animals which you show her, making their sound.

TOUCH	• Stacking blocks covered in interesting textures. • Any objects of different textures. • Teething rings.
MOVEMENT	• Swings and spandex or lycra hammocks. • Never leave your baby unsupervised in a swing or hammock.
MOTOR DEVELOPMENT	• Commercial pram toys are fun for travel time and encourage a variety of fine motor functions. • Wooden cubes. • Balls.

WALKING RINGS

They keep baby out of mischief for a while. They free your hands to cook dinner or wash up. But are they really such a good idea? There are two important reasons why a walking ring should not be used:

THEY CONTRIBUTE TO FALLS

As your baby whizzes along on the floor, she may hit a bump which causes rapid deceleration. This, plus the top-heavy distribution of her weight in the walking-ring makes tip-over accidents highly likely. In the USA, tipping over of walking rings is one of the biggest causes of head injuries in babies in the first year of life.

THEY HAMPER DEVELOPMENT

Walking rings are most often used at a stage when your baby should be practising the skills needed for crawling. They not only hamper the development of crawling on a motor level, but also diminish the motivation to crawl, as baby can get where she wants to by means of the ring. In addition, the supported standing position has a negative effect on the development of the hips, legs and feet as weight-bearing limbs for walking.

If you are determined to use a walking ring, don't use it as a babysitter. Use it in moderation – no more than ten minutes a day, and with constant supervision. A better option is a push trolley or the new generation of stationary rings.

BABY'S FINE – HOW ARE YOU?

See page 103 if you think you may be suffering from perinatal distress.

Eggy bread

To soft-boiled egg yolk, add a dash of Bovril/Marmite to taste, ½ slice of crumbled bread or toast with the crusts cut off, and ½ teaspoon of grated cheese. For variety, add a small pinch of ground almonds, sesame or pumpkin seeds.

As an alternative, make scrambled egg (add a splash of formula milk or water to dilute the egg a bit), top with ½ teaspoon of grated cheese and a small pinch of ground sesame or pumpkin seeds.

To make French toast, dip a slice of bread in a mixture of egg, formula milk and grated cheese. Lightly fry in sesame/olive oil or butter, and serve – either mushy or crisp and cut into fingers (as a finger food).

Chicken broth

Soak 2 cups each of barley and lentils overnight in enough water to cover them – rinse and drain. Place a whole chicken, including giblets and livers, with approximately 2-3 litres of water into a large pot. Add lentils and barley and bring to the boil. Simmer for 3-4 hours, until the meat falls off the bone, and the lentils and barley are soft. You may need to add extra water as it simmers. (If you are using a pressure cooker, boil for 20 minutes.) Remove carcass and skin, and purée the broth left behind. This makes a rich protein broth, which can be frozen. Serve with freshly cooked vegetables.

Fish bake

Cook any type of pasta until soft. Place in a casserole dish. Add a layer of pilchards or sardines, or semi-cooked hake or kingklip. Mix an egg into 100 ml of formula or full cream milk and pour over fish. Cover with grated cheese or chunky cottage cheese. Bake for approximately 20 minutes at 180 ºC. If you don't want to use formula or full cream milk, substitute with mashed pumpkin or butternut. The size of the casserole dish used will determine quantities of the ingredients.

If you wish to freeze cooked portions, don't add the cheese – only add it when you heat up a defrosted portion.

For variation use minced chicken or beef instead of fish.

White sauce

Add 1 egg to 200 ml formula milk. Bring to the boil over low heat. Add 1 tablespoon grated cheese and stir. Slowly add 1 tablespoon of cornflour to thicken the mixture, stirring continuously to prevent lumps. Spoon this protein-rich sauce over mashed potato, cooked pasta, cooked corn rice, or any steamed vegetables. This is a most useful way to get your baby to take more formula milk if she is a picky drinker.

Vegetable soup

Soak 2 cups each of lentils, barley and white kidney beans overnight in enough water to cover them – rinse and drain. Place 2 cups chopped seasonal vegetables in a pot, with 2-3 litres of water. Add soaked lentils, barley and beans. Bring to the boil, turn down heat and simmer until soft (1-2 hours in a normal pot, 15 minutes in a pressure cooker).

Serve with a slice of crumbled bread or toast (remove the crusts). Grate 1 teaspoon of cheese over, or add a pinch of ground almonds, or pumpkin or sesame seeds.

Avocado, banana and cottage cheese

Mash ripe avocado pear, banana (or any other soft fresh fruit) and 1 teaspoon of cottage cheese together. Add a liberal pinch of brown sugar to taste. A drop or two of Worcestershire sauce, or a very small amount of Marmite/Bovril can be added instead of the sugar to add variety to the diet. Serve the mash as is, or spread onto crustless bread/toast and cut into cubes/fingers as a finger food.

It can also be served as a dip for a year-old toddler with sesame sticks, cheese straws, toast or soft crackers.

Bean casserole

Soak 2 cups of kidney, mung or sugar beans overnight in enough water to cover the beans – rinse and drain. Brown 1 chopped onion in a little sesame or olive oil. Add 2 cups of soaked beans or 1 cup of cooked chick-peas. Cover with boiling water and simmer for about an hour (10 minutes in a pressure cooker).

Add some chopped carrots, 1 chopped fresh tomato or ½ cup tomato puree and chopped parsley to taste. Add more boiling water to fill pot to about 3 cm above the bean and vegetable mixture. Cook for another hour (or 10 minutes in the pressure cooker).

Place ¼ cup of cashew nuts or sunflower seeds with ½ cup of water in a food processor and blend till smooth. Use 1 tablespoon of cashew-nut butter instead of blending your own. Add blended nuts or cashew-nut butter to stew. If necessary, thicken with cornflour, stirring continuously to prevent lumps. Add ¼ teaspoon of brown sugar or molasses to taste. Serve with corn or brown rice .

Unthickened, this can also be served as a soup, with 1 slice of crustless bread or toast crumbled into it.

For variation, replace beans or chickpeas with 2 cups of soaked lentils. Omit the blended cashew nuts or cashew-nut butter and sprinkle with crushed pumpkin seeds instead.

Nine to twelve months

Your baby is entering the most exciting (and, for you, exhausting) phase of his first year of development. He is becoming mobile and is discovering what an exciting place his world is.

By now, he should be able to sit well on his own and will show an active interest in retrieving objects that move out of his reach. This is the age when separation anxiety starts, and he will exasperate you with his fickleness of mood. One minute he will be playing quite happily on his own, and the next he will be sobbing inconsolably if you move out of his line of vision.

FEEDING

If you have delayed introducing solids from all food groups until this point, it is very important that you do so now. It is of the utmost importance that you include protein in your baby's diet and reduce the number of milk feeds offered. If you are following the feeding routine as recommended in the previous chapter, keep going.

Solid food

Increase his portions according to his demands. He should now be having in the region of a cup (250 ml) of solid food per meal. Bear in mind that his appetite will vary from day to day, so don't worry if he eats less than this from time to time. If your baby is not allergic, you can introduce cooked egg-white to his diet. Do this slowly over a few days, starting with half a teaspoon and gradually increasing the quantity.

Most of the time, he can eat what the rest of the family is eating, provided it's a balanced diet. Introduce more texture to his food by making it coarser. You no longer need to purée it, except for certain fibrous textures like cooked meat or chicken. Rather mash his food with the back of a fork. Start experimenting with different tastes, like adding a little garlic, tomato or onion to his food. Don't worry if he spits out or gags when you introduce something new. It's normal.

Don't despair when your baby plunges his entire fist into his bowl of food. These attempts to feed himself are a wonderful sensory and developmental experience. Continue giving him finger food, but avoid anything that will break off into hard pieces and not soften once in the mouth.

Don't forget about iron and plant protein supplements (see page 129).

Milk feeds

Keep your baby on breast or formula milk in addition to solids until he is one year old. Continue to add formula milk to his cereal. If he's losing interest in his milk feed after lunch, don't force him to have it. If his diet is balanced, he doesn't need it. If he still enjoys it, make sure it doesn't spoil his appetite for dinner.

He will soon have two milk feeds a day of 250 ml each – the first when he wakes in the morning and the second after supper, before bedtime. Don't be tempted to stop formula milk and start him on cow's milk as it is low in vitamins A, D and C, and especially in iron. You may use cow's milk for cooking, for example, in scrambled egg or mashed potato. Don't give your baby low-fat or fat-free milk or dairy products. He needs sufficient fats and cholesterol in his diet for the growth and development of his brain and to ensure an adequate energy intake.

Moving on to a feeding cup

Offer your baby his mid-morning and mid-afternoon water, juice or tea in a feeding cup with a spout or straw. Use a feeding cup with handles on both sides so that he can hold it himself. Don't worry if he appears not to have a clue how to actually use it – with time he will work it out. Invest in a non-spill cup to avoid hours of carpet mopping.

Continue to give him his morning and evening milk feeds in a standard feeding bottle with a teat.

MORE TEETH

First the central and then the lateral incisors make their appearance. By one year he should have four top teeth and four bottom teeth. If he is biting your nipple during breast-feeding, let him know that it is not acceptable by removing the nipple immediately from his mouth, admonishing him in a stern voice.

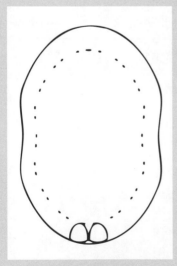

Lower central incisors
(6-9 months)

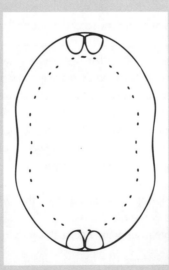

Top central incisors
(6-9 months)

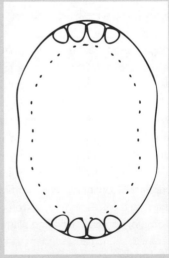

Lateral incisors
(by 12 months)

- Make your house and garden child proof with regard to objects and sub-stances that could harm your baby. He can drown in just a few centime-tres of water, so don't leave water in buckets, basins and baths. Securely fence off the swimming pool and cover ornamental ponds or bird baths in the garden.
- Once he is mobile, ensure he is supervised. You will be amazed at how much damage he can do to himself – and your possessions – in the shortest amount of time!
- Keep coffee-table tops clear, watch out for electrical cords hanging down, and cover all accessible plug points.
- Get into the habit of keeping the bathroom door closed at all times.
- Keep all your cleaning substances in high cupboards.
- Remove wobbly furniture which he can easily pull down on top of himself.
- Keep the garage door firmly locked. As an extra precaution, place all pesti-cides, fertilizers, petrol, tools, etc. on high shelves. Pick up small nails, nuts and bolts lying on the garage floor. Keep your baby away from automated garage doors.
- If you have stairs, invest in a stair guard or fit pool netting across the opening.

SLEEP

Your baby no longer needs to eat or drink just before bedtime, so try not to let him associate going to bed with feeding. He should sleep for 10 to 12 hours a night without requiring a feed, so don't be tempted to feed him if he wakes during the night.

If he continues to wake during the night, go through the process of elimination to exclude any specific causes, then teach him how to go back to sleep by himself (see page 53). Bear in mind that he may experience separation anxiety at this age, so give him plenty of attention during the day, and perhaps an extra hug and cuddle at bedtime. Expect some restless nights whilst he is teething.

Now that he is mobile, he can become over-stimulated very quickly and this may disturb his sleep habits. Make sure he is in a calming environment before sleep time.

FLEXIBLE ROUTINE FOR NINE TO TWELVE MONTHS

- Your baby should now be eating solids from all food groups spread between breakfast, lunch and supper with small snacks mid-morning and afternoon.
- He may drop his after-lunch milk feed and may only want milk when waking in the morning and after supper.
- Your baby will sleep for 10 to 12 hours at night without needing a feed.
- Limit his awake time to 2 to 3 hours between sleeps and plan your care-

giving, outings and stimulation within this time.
- He will be having one to three sleeps during the day, varying from 40 minutes to two hours in length.
- He should be sleeping for 14 to 15 hours in a 24-hour cycle.

WHAT'S BABY UP TO?

At this stage locomotion is the name of the game. Whether he's a really fast crawler or a precocious walker, your baby will be all over the place and the term 'war zone' takes on a whole new meaning. Being mobile is important for the development of spatial awareness and as of now your little one starts to map his world.

His vision is well developed and he can follow a rapidly moving object. Books are a firm favourite and he'll sit still to be read to.

From sitting to walking

Your baby has been enjoying extended periods of sitting unsupported on the floor. In this position he'll really start developing his fine motor skills, but as he gets closer to a year, sitting becomes too static and he'll only use it if exploring something interesting or as a transitory position before moving off into crawling again or pulling himself up to stand.

He begins to pull himself to a standing position in earnest. Any person, animal or piece of furniture will be a leaning post. He'll land with a bump on his backside in order to get back to the floor. When he's standing, it isn't long before he will start to rock on his legs while holding on to something. Then one day, one of those rockings will become a step and soon thereafter he'll be cruising along at a rate of knots, holding on to the furniture.

Cruising is the vital stage before walking and can continue until after a year of age. Walking is the most variable milestone and should not be used as a gauge of developmental success unless there are other indicators of giftedness or serious delay. Some babies start walking at nine months and others only at sixteen months.

Dexterity and language

Your baby will start using his hands as useful tools. He can give you a toy and will practise accurately releasing it. He can point his index finger and he pokes at small objects and holes. Mouthing decreases at this stage as he actively starts to manipulate and explore objects with his hands. He uses his fingers to feed himself, chewing on biscuits and holding his own bottle and 'sippy' cup.

He also starts to use language to communicate, understanding more than you'd believe. He loves to imitate noises, such as a cough. He will also babble loudly, doubling up syllables into 'ga-ga' or 'ba-ba', for example. He may even say a few real words by the time he is a year old. 'Da-da' usually comes first – it's easier to say than 'ma-ma'. A deaf child's vocalizations will now differ from those of a hearing child, as they remain sparse and monotonous.

Your baby's sense of humour is developing rapidly and he becomes really affectionate towards you. He loves games such as clapping hands and waving bye-bye. But his mood will turn in a second if you try removing a favourite toy from him or taking him away from dangerous situations. Now he shows that 'will of his own'.

ENHANCING DEVELOPMENT

Encourage your baby to move from a sitting position by placing interesting toys out of his reach. Encourage him to crawl and provide opportunities for him to explore. Understand his frustration when you remove him from a potentially dangerous situation that he is happily exploring and offer an alternative source of entertainment that has the added advantage of safety.

To encourage cruising, position pieces of furniture at just the right distance apart. Tell him plenty of stories that teach him about his body and take him on lots of outings during his awake times as he now wants to learn about the world around him.

A sensory diet

This is a really enjoyable stage, when your baby actively seeks stimulation and is also able to integrate it better. Outings and mother and baby playgroups become really worthwhile, as he expands his world.

ENVIRONMENT

Now your baby actively explores his environment. Because he can regulate his states well and does not become easily overloaded, you can increase the amount of stimulation he receives. By now you will know his temperament and his threshold for sensory input. If he is a fussy baby who is easily over-stimulated, adjust the sensory input accordingly.

• Provide sensible clothing for crawling and rolling.
• In each room have a baby-toy basket. These toys will help to keep your baby occupied as you move from room to room during the day. Choose a sensory

theme for each room, for instance lounge – smell toys, kitchen – sound toys, bathroom – touch toys. Or each basket can have one toy to stimulate each sense, for instance a smelly toy, a noisy toy, a feely toy and a bright visual toy.

ROUTINE-RELATED ACTIVITIES (TIMING)

Include stimulating activities and calming strategies in your daily care-giving programme. Stimulating activities will feature prominently, but calming remains important in view of the increased stimulating input.

SLEEP TIME

A calm sleep environment is still important – as his senses take in more information, it becomes harder to switch off and go to sleep at bedtime.

SIGHT	• If your baby is sleeping well and is not fractious during the day, livening up the décor of his room should not affect his sleeping patterns.
MOTOR DEVELOPMENT	• Your baby is now mobile enough to choose his own sleep position. If he chooses to sleep on his tummy, don't worry – the risk of SIDS has decreased and you will disturb his sleep if you turn him back each time he rolls onto his tummy.

NAPPY CHANGE TIME

Nappy change time continues to be a challenge, as your baby dislikes being on his back. Provide toys to distract him, so that you can get the nappy change over and done with.

SIGHT	• Keep a variety of bright pictures to hand to him or place above the changing mat. Photographs of family members or pets in plastic slip-in frames will keep him entertained while you complete the dreaded task.
HEARING	• Talk to him about the pictures or the people or pets in the photographs.

BATH TIME

Bath time remains the start of the bedtime routine, so don't over-excite your baby. Rather play quietly and then be very calm after his bath.

SIGHT	• Waterproof books are fun for bath time.
HEARING	• Sing songs and recite nursery rhymes describing his body.

Touch	• Teach your baby the qualities of toys: heavy and light, sink and float. • Enhance body image by touching parts of the body, labelling them for your baby: "These are your toes" or "Let's wash your tummy". • Introduce a new texture at bath time by spraying shaving-foam onto the tiles next to the bath or onto the sides of the bath.
Motor development	• Let him stand at the bath to be undressed, which encourages cruising.
Smell	• He will enjoy scented bubble bath and other fragrant baby bath products.

Awake time

Most of your day is filled with running around after an active, awake baby. Enjoy this time by stimulating him with various activities.

Sight	• Show him moving things such as birds flying and trees swaying in the wind, to encourage visual tracking. • Blow bubbles for him to watch as they drift off, encouraging visual tracking. • Play hiding games, hiding toys for him to find. • Babies love to see themselves in the mirror. Point out his body parts as he gazes at his reflection.
Hearing	• On outings talk about what you see, for example animals and the noises they make. • Talk about the things your baby shows an interest in. Speak to him all the time, labelling events, feelings and objects.
Touch	• Touch things you see outdoors, such as flowers and animals. • In the warm summer months, set up large tubs with a variety of textured substances: water, jelly, sand, balls of all sizes. Make this a weekly, shared experience with friends and their babies, changing the substances each week. • Sing and act out touch songs such as 'This little piggy'. • Keep several touch objects in each room of the house for him to play with.
Movement	• Rough-and-tumble games are fun with babies of this age. • Go to the park and let him play on moving equipment such as seesaws, swings and slides.

MOTOR DEVELOPMENT	• To encourage eye-hand co-ordination, suspend a balloon in front of him so that he can catch it as it floats slowly by, allowing time for him to plan the action. As he improves, make it more difficult by using a ball in a stocking. • Give him a large ball to throw, gradually moving on to smaller ones. Let him throw toys into a basket. • Play ring-on-a-stick games to encourage purposeful release. Take a stick and give him a ring to place over the stick. • In the kitchen, have pots or plastic containers that can be stacked up. He will do this enthusiastically, now that his release skill is well developed. Let him unpack your cupboards with pots and plastic ware and teach him how putting everything back can be fun too. • Make an obstacle course with cushions and tables and baskets for him to crawl in, out and under and use any old boxes to make tunnels and hidey holes which babies love to explore. • Encourage crawling by giving him pushing and moving toys and by crawling over him when he crawls. • Let him crawl up a slide or incline to help develop his shoulder muscles. • Teach your baby to go down steps backwards. • To encourage standing and cruising, place interesting objects on chest height surfaces. Also, first place furniture close together and progressively move it further apart. • Let your baby push a block trolley to assist his progression to walking. • To encourage walking as he gets closer to a year, play the '1, 2, 3, weeee!' game: he walks between mom and dad, holding your hands; each time he takes a step, count '1, 2, 3' and then swing him in the air on 'weee!'.

TRAVELLING TIME

Travelling can be a very frustrating time for your busy mover. He will protest at being strapped into his car seat and stimulation is often essential to make a trip bearable.

SIGHT	• Attach a toy-on-elastic to the grab-handle above the window so that your baby can pull it towards himself to play with. Alternate between squeaky toys, touch toys and a book.

HEARING	• Continue to play CDs of children's singing. Teach your baby the actions in action songs at home and he will keep himself happily occupied by doing them in the car.
MOVEMENT	• Carry him in a back-pack carrier when going on walks. He will love the movement and seeing the world from this vantage point.

FEED TIME

Meal times can be a challenge, as your baby's new-found desire to feed himself coupled with inadequate motor skills leave him covered in food. Place a plastic sheet under his highchair and give him his own spoon at meal times, then relax about the floor and feed him with another spoon.

TOUCH	• Even though it's messy, allow your baby to feed himself – experiencing different food textures is a wonderful and important learning opportunity.
MOTOR DEVELOPMENT	• Give him finger food in a variety of shapes and sizes to encourage the development of grip and finger dexterity.
SMELL	• Encourage awareness of various aromas by pointing out the sweet smell of vanilla, the fresh smell of citrus and the savoury aroma of a stew.

TOYS AND TOOLS

The range of toys available for this age is staggering. Don't spoil your baby with loads of toys, though, as he will get as much enjoyment and benefit from playing with household objects. If he has lots of toys, put some away and rotate the collection. That way there is always something new and interesting.

SIGHT	• Lift-the-flap board books will fascinate and involve him.
HEARING	• CDs and tapes of children's singing and nursery rhymes. • Musical toys – anything from the wide range available, for instance a ring-stacker with a separate tune playing for each ring which is stacked.
TOUCH	• Books with touch components: different textures for different animals or objects will help to develop his sense of touch.
MOVEMENT	• Playground equipment such as swings and seesaws are great at this age.

MOTOR DEVELOPMENT	• Sturdy push-along toys. • Toys to encourage fine motor control, for example activity centres or toys with holes to encourage pointing and poking. • Make him a fabric book with each page featuring and item that requires fine motor control (a Velcro strip, button, press stud and so on). • Thick wax crayons and paper. • Open-and-close toys are popular at this age.

OPTIMIZE DEVELOPMENT

To ensure your baby's continued health, well-being and optimal development:
• Follow a sense-able feeding plan.
• Establish good sleep habits.
• Stick to your flexible routine.
• Implement the sense-able secrets you've learnt.
• Use the TEAT framework for a sensory diet.

Recommended reading as your baby becomes a toddler:
Toddler Sense by Ann Richardson (Metz Press, 2005)

Recommended reading for sleep problems:
Sleep Sense by Megan Faure and Ann Richardson (Metz Press, 2007)

BABY'S FINE – HOW ARE YOU?

See page 103 if you think you may be suffering from perinatal distress.

CRITERIA TO IDENTIFY BABIES WITH REGULATORY DISORDERS & DIFFICULTIES PROCESSING SENSORY INPUT

Some children are particularly sensitive to sensory input and do not integrate it adequately. This can lead to extreme fussing, poor sleep habits, feeding problems and emotional irritability. If you are concerned that your baby is significantly more irritable than average and may have a problem with processing sensory input, you should work through this checklist. If your baby is over six months of age and shows at least two of the following signs, you may wish to have him assessed by an occupational therapist who treats babies and is specialized in sensory integration to ascertain whether he has a regulatory disorder.

Distress with routine care-giving and play experiences involving a sensory experience

Your baby may respond by crying, withdrawal, or other negative behaviours when confronted with normal everyday sensory stimulation involving touch, movement, sight and hearing.

TOUCH
- Resists cuddling, pulls away or arches
- Resists being swaddled
- Distressed at having face or hair washed
- Distressed by being dressed or undressed and may prefer being naked or be happier in many layers or very warm clothes
- Distressed when strapped into car seat
- Avoids touching certain textures or getting hands messy

MOVEMENT
- Distressed when swung in the air or involved in boisterous play
- Resists being placed in certain positions (for example on back or stomach)
- Doesn't crawl before walking

SIGHT
- Sensitive to bright lights – cries or closes eyes
- Avoids eye contact and turns away from people's faces
- Becomes overly excited in noisy, bustling settings such as a crowded supermarket or restaurant

HEARING
- Is startled or distressed by loud sounds (such as a door bell or barking dog)
- No or very little babbling or vocalising

Sleep disturbances

This is a persistent problem in the regulation of sleep-wake cycles, and involves difficulties in falling asleep and staying asleep, which are not associated with parenting style.
- Takes over 30 minutes to fall asleep, even after calming techniques and bed-time routines have been implemented.
- Wakes frequently (more than twice) during the night for reasons other than hunger or age appropriate night-feeds.

Difficulty self-calming

Your baby is unable to self-calm by bringing hands to mouth, looking at calming images, or listening to calming voices or sounds. Once upset, he requires extreme efforts to calm down. If you spend more than three hours a day over a period of three weeks or longer attempting to calm your baby, it is more than normal unsettledness and may indicate a regulatory disorder.

Feeding difficulties

Your baby may be suffering from a feeding disorder if at least two of the following apply:
- Had difficulty latching for more than five days as a newborn.
- Does not tolerate the change from breast to a rubber or silicone teat.
- Does not have an established, regular feeding schedule.
- Demonstrates distress around the process of feeding, with regurgitation and spitting out of food, particularly when eating textured or lumpy foods.
- Is extremely fussy about texture and prefers only smooth foods.

Distress with changes in routine

Your baby becomes very disorganized if her normal daily routine is disrupted or by transitions from one activity to the next. This is manifested by prolonged periods of crying or fussing (over five minutes) that occur at least three times per day.

Emotional instability

Your baby is generally fussy, irritable and unhappy and tends to change rapidly from contented to distressed without any apparent reason. In many cases these behaviours are very disruptive to the family. Your baby is never very happy and does not initiate interaction with you (over nine months).

(Adapted from DeGangi et al 1996 *Criteria for inclusion in research*)

BREAST-FEEDING SUPPLEMENT
Express breast milk successfully

Ensuring an adequate supply of expressed breast milk to sustain your baby's needs takes commitment and perseverance. Expressing breast milk for the feeds that you miss while you are at work (or otherwise absent) will help to maintain milk supply for the breast-feeds that you can give (for example early morning and/or evening), based on the principle of supply and demand.

Your working conditions will play an important role in determining whether you can, in fact, express breast-milk every few hours during your working day. The simple difference between having a private office or being a sales representative out on the road may well be the deciding factor.

- Ideally, always try to express milk throughout the day when it would be time for your baby to feed. This will ensure adequate milk supply.
- Time permitting, try to express milk after a feed when you are at home. This is when the richer hindmilk has been released. This milk is more fat and carbohydrate-rich than the foremilk and will be more satisfying for your baby.
- Try to keep up your fluid intake during the day (at least two litres).
- Double pumping (both breasts at the same time) has been shown to increase the fat content, as well as the amount of milk.
- If a regular schedule is difficult to manage, try to express at least once during your working day. Lunch time is usually a good time – put your feet up, have a bite to eat and read a magazine.
- Always allow the freshly expressed breast-milk to cool before refrigerating it (if you have an office fridge), or placing it in a sealed cooler box – stored in a cool place.
- If you have no refrigeration facilities at work, or you are on the road, consider investing in a good quality cooler box. Some top-of-the-range breast pumps come complete with accessories such as specialized cooler bags to store expressed milk.
- Breast milk can be stored in the fridge for 24 hours and frozen for up to three months.
- Freeze expressed milk into washed and sterilized ice trays or small plastic juice bottle containers – specialized plastic bags are also available.
- Always express milk into a sterilized 'non-glass' container as the antibodies present in breast milk stick to glass and are left behind when the bottle is emptied. Most pumps come complete with specialized, non-glass containers to express into.
- Thaw frozen milk by standing the plastic container in a jug of warm water to defrost.
- Don't microwave expressed breast milk – this may destroy much of the milk's nutritional value.
- Always sterilize all the parts of the pump, including the container, thoroughly.
- Discard any unused, refrigerated milk after 24 hours.

Since milk supply fluctuates you may find that you have more milk on a Monday because you have been feeding more often over the weekend. By Friday, your milk supply may be reduced, because breast-feeds were fewer during the week.

Two ways to wean
'COLD TURKEY'
This describes the process of replacing all breast-feeds with formula feeds within a period of 24 hours. This usually happens when you have simply had enough, or other circumstances prevail, preventing you from continuing with breast-feeding, for example illness or trauma, or the toxic effects of certain medication.

We recommend that you ask your pharmacist for medication that inhibits the release of certain milk-producing hormones. In addition, anti-inflammatory and pain-relieving medication can be taken orally in tablet form, or rubbed directly onto the breasts in cream form. In some instances, a mild diuretic is prescribed to relieve water retention. Seek your pharmacist's advice.

Cold cabbage leaves – placed inside your bra and replaced frequently when they start 'cooking' – are a wonderful folk remedy that really works! Wear a firm bra with support, but don't bind your breasts with bandages.

If you are in great discomfort, it is absolutely acceptable to express off 'the tip of the iceberg' three to four times a day. This means to express your breasts until you are comfortable, not until they are soft and empty. Discard this milk if you are on medication, but keep it for your baby if you are not. You may have to do this for up to about a week or 10 days, gradually decreasing the frequency and the amount of time spent expressing.

Watch out for signs of mastitis (inflammation of the mammary glands), such as red, swollen, lumpy breasts with associated chills, fever and flu-like symptoms. Massage Arnica cream or an anti-inflammatory cream onto identifiable swollen, red areas, which may be caused by a blocked milk duct, and keep cold compresses on the affected breast to reduce swelling. (A small packet of frozen peas is very useful!)

A fairly rare complication of 'cold turkey' weaning may be the formation of a breast abscess as a result of untreated mastitis. Seek professional medical help. You will need antibiotic medication and, in some cases, drainage of the abscess.

GRADUAL WEANING
Begin by replacing one breast-feed of the day with a formula feed. The 10 am feed is usually a good one to start with. Never offer the breast at this time again. If you can, wait until the next breast-feed is due, and proceed to breast-feed as usual. If you are very uncomfortable, gently rub some Arnica cream onto your breast and place a cold compress or cabbage leaf in your bra. Resist the temptation to express milk but if you simply have to, only express until you are comfortable, not until the breast is empty.

Within 72 hours the lack of demand for a breast-feed at that specific time will significantly alter the production of milk for that feed and you should no longer experience any discomfort. On day three (not before), or whenever you are ready to drop another feed, proceed as before. But do not choose a feed directly after the first feed you dropped – try with the late afternoon feed this time.

On day six (not before) or whenever you are ready to drop another feed, proceed as before. This time try with the lunchtime breast-feed. On day nine (not before), or again when you are ready, stop the bedtime breast-feed. By day 12 (not before), or when you are ready, stop the only breast-feed left, namely the early morning feed. If you proceed slowly, the production of your breast-milk will slowly decrease, according to supply and demand, with less risk of breast engorgement, mastitis and abscess formation.

Starting again
Weaning may be achieved within 24 hours, or it may take up to a year. Your individual circumstances and needs will determine exactly how long it will take. If you change your mind about weaning or your circumstances change, it is very easy to relactate, even if you have stopped breast-feeding for a few weeks. Ask your clinic sister to help you re-establish breast-feeding.

NURSERY RHYMES

Nursery rhymes are a wonderfully enjoyable way to enhance language development. Adding actions to rhymes makes them fun for your baby and teaches him about his body parts through touch and movement. He also learns to anticipate actions, and develops a concept of sequences. Always watch for positive reactions to touch and movement, as sharing rhymes must be fun in order to enhance the bonding process.

This little piggy

This little piggy went to market,
This little piggy stayed at home,
This little piggy had roast beef,
This little piggy had none.
And this little piggy cried "Wee-wee-wee" all the way home.

As you say this rhyme, pull each toe or finger in turn. At the end, run your fingers up his arm or leg and tickle him on his tummy.

Pat-a-cake

Pat-a-cake, pat-a-cake, baker's man,
Bake me a cake as fast as you can,
Pat it and prick it and mark it with 'B',
And put it in the oven for baby and me.

Clap your baby's hands together as you say this rhyme. On the third line pretend to prick your baby's hand and draw a B on her hand.

Row, row, row, your boat

Row, row, row, your boat, gently down the stream,
Merrily, merrily, merrily, merrily, life is but a dream.

Rock your baby backwards and forwards as you sing this rhyme.

Rock-a-bye-baby

Rock-a-bye-baby, on the tree top,
When the wind blows the cradle will rock.
When the bough breaks, the cradle will fall.
And down will come baby, cradle and all.

Rock your baby in your arms and on the third line pretend to drop him by tilting him backwards quickly.

Ride a cockhorse

Ride a cockhorse to Banbury Cross
To see a fine lady upon a white horse.
With rings on her fingers and bells on her toes
She shall have music wherever she goes.

Sit your baby on your lap and bounce her up and down until the third line when you point out her fingers and her toes.

Sing this rhyme to him,
pausing just before the
"POP", to give him a feeling
of anticipation just before a
little fright.

POP goes the weasel

Half a pound of tuppenny rice
Half a pound of treacle
That's the way the money goes
POP goes the weasel!

This is the way the lady rides

This is the way the lady rides
Trit, trot, trit, trot, trit, trot.
This is the way the gentleman rides
Gallop-a-hop, gallop-a-hop.
This is the way the old man rides
Hobbledy-gig, hobbledy-gig,
And into the ditch he falls.

Jiggle your baby up and
down on your knee, varying
the rhythm for each rider.
Pretend to drop her into a
ditch on the last line.

Round and round the garden

Round and round the garden,
Like a teddy bear.
One-step, two-step, tickle you under there.

Walk your fingers round the
palm of his hand and on the
third line walk your fingers
up his arm and tickle him
under the armpit.

Rub-a-dub-dub

Rub-a-dub-dub
Three men in a tub
Who do you think they are?
The butcher, the baker, the candlestick maker
All jumped out of a rotten potato
Turn them out, knaves all three.

Start the rhyme in a quiet
voice and pause expectantly
after the third line. Then,
in a louder voice, say the
fourth line.

Incy Wincy spider

Incy Wincy spider went climbing up the spout.
Down came the rain and washed the spider out.
Out came the sun and dried up all the rain.
So Incy Wincy spider went climbing up again.

With the first line, show a
spider climbing upwards;
second line, wiggle fingers
to show rain falling down;
third line, show a circle with
your arms above your head;
fourth line, show spider
climbing up again.

REFERENCES AND RECOMMENDED READING

Als, H. *A synactive model of neonatal behavioural organization*, 1986

Bailey K. *Making sense of my world. Stimulating sensory & motor development in babies.* Video series Part 1-4

Baldwin Dancy R. *You Are Your Child's First Teacher.* Berkeley, CA: Celestial Arts, 1989

Chauke HL, *Baby Talk* Professional Forum South Africa: October 2009

DeGangi G. *Pediatric Disorders of Regulation in Affect and Behaviour.* San Diego, CA: Academic Press, 2000

DeGangi G, Wiener A, Long T, Battaile B. *Sensory Processing of Infants Born Prematurely or with Regulatory Disorders.* Physical &
    Occupational Therapy in Pediatrics Vol. 16(4), 1996

Dennill K. *Meeting maternal and child survival targets in South Africa through prevention of mother-to-child transmission of HIV.* PNT Jour-
    nal of Nursing, November/December 2008

Du Plessis D. *Pocket guide to breast-feeding*: Cape Town: Juta & co, 2008.

Einon D. *Learning Early.* London: Marshall Publishing, 1998

Eliot L. *What's Going On In There.* New York, NY: Bantam Books, 1999

Eliott L, Henderson J, Northstone K et al. *Prospective study of breast feeding in relation to wheeze, atopy and
    bronchial hyperresponsiveness* in the ALSPAC Journal Allergy Clinical Immunology, 2008

Evanoo G. MS. *Infant Crying: A Clinical Conundrum* in RN Journal of Pediatric Health Care, Sept/Oct 2007

Faure M. & Richardson A. *Sleep sense.* Welgemoed: Metz Press, 2007

Field T, Field Tory, Cullen C et al. *Lavender bath oil reduces stress and crying and enhances sleep in very young infants.* Touch Research
    Institute, Fielding Graduate University, Duke University School of Medicine, USA: October 2007

Host A, Halken S, Muraro A et al. *Dietary prevention of allergic diseases in infants and small children.* Paediatric
    Allergy Immunology, 2008

Hussey-Gardner B. *Understanding my signals.* VORT Corporation, 1996

Jansen J, Beijers R et al. *Cortisol reactivity in young infants*: Department of Developmental Pshychology, Radboud
    University, Nijmegen, Netherlands: July 2009

Kitzinger S. *Breast-feeding.* London: Dorling Kindersley, 1998

Kitzinger S. *The Crying Baby.* London: Viking, 1989

Krantz M. *Child Development.* Belmont, CA: Wadsworth, 1994

Murkoff H. *The Real Parenting Expert is … You.* Newsweek Special 2000 Edition

Murray-Slutsky C & Paris B. *Exploring the Spectrum of Autism and Pervasive Developmental Disorders.*
    San Antonio, Texas: Therapy Skill Builders, 2000

National Center for Clinical Infant Programs. *Diagnostic Classification of Mental Health and Developmental disorders of Infancy and
    Early Childhood: Zero to Three*, 1994

Natural Health Association SA. *Mother and Baby Essentials – a practical guide*, 1999

Nusing Update Magazine South Africa. *Aids is not a death sentence.* November 2009

OT week. *Fussy Babies.* Dec 1991

Paller A, Hornung R et al. *Infant skin and its special needs –* Johnson & Johnson Compendium of Infant Skin Care, 2001

Perrins, M. *Normal Development.* NDT and SI workshop, Wynberg Military Hospital, March 1991

Raymond J. *Kids, Start your Engines.* Newsweek Special 2000 Edition

Richardson A. *Toddler sense.* Welgemoed: Metz Press, 2005

Roley S.S. *Neurophysiological Benefits of the Baby Sling.* Unpublished article, 1992

Sammons W. *The Self-Calmed Baby.* New York: St. Martins, 1989

Schaffer R. *Mothering.* London: Fontana, 1977

Sheridan M.D. *From Birth to Five Years.* London: Routledge, 1991

Sicherer S.H. & Burks A.W. *Maternal and infant diets for prevention of allergic diseases: understanding menu changes in 2008.*
    Journal Allergy Clinical Immunology, 2008

Stoppard M. *New Parent.* London: Dorling Kindersley, 1999

Stoppard M. *Complete Baby & Child Care.* London: Dorling Kindersley, 2001

Stoppard M. *Know Your Child.* London: Dorling Kindersley, 1991

Thygarajan A. & Burks A. *AAP recommendations on the effects of early nutritional interventions on the development of atopic disease.*
    Current Opinion in Pediatrics, 2008

Turner R. & Nanayakkara S. *The soothing art of baby massage.* London: Chancellor Press, 1996

Vergara, Elsie R. ScD. OTR TOPSEI: *Overview of neonatal intervention.*